I0831071

ONCE UPON A COOKBOOK

THIS BOOK BELONGS TO

ONCE UPON A COOKBOOK

A Treasury of Recipes Inspired by Timeless Children's Books

Written by Bryton Taylor

Illustrated by Emma Adams

SAN RAFAEL • LOS ANGELES • LONDON

Contents

6
Introduction

9
The Breakfast Table

31
Morning and Afternoon Tea

53
Picnics and Light Luncheons

73
Hearty Meals

95
Traditional Treats

113
Delightful Sips

128
Suggested Menus

130
Fry Station Safety

131
Dietary Considerations

132
Measurement Conversions

135
Acknowledgments

136
Index

Introduction

Every book has the power to transport us, but childhood favorites hold a particular kind of magic. When we return to them as adults—whether for nostalgia's sake or to share them with a new generation—they welcome us back like dear old friends, as if no time has passed at all.

No sooner would I turn a page in *The Wind in the Willows* would I feel the sunshine and fresh spring breeze alongside Mole before embarking on an idyllic picnic, with a basket brimming with cold meats, cress sandwiches, and refreshing lemonade, after rowing steadily down the river with Rat. When I revisited *The House at Pooh Corner*, I would find Piglet beckoning to me from inside the Hundred Acre Wood and age would fade away as we searched through a friend's cupboard alongside Winnie-the-Pooh with a rumbly tummy, satisfyingly dipping our sticky paws into honey and condensed milk. Time slips away—half an hour, an hour. I would lift my head in surprise, finding myself back in the room where I had begun. Curiosity would get the better of me, just like Tigger, to know: What *is* that strengthening medicine Roo had?

The books referred to in this cookbook come from what is now known as the golden age of children's literature, spanning from the mid-nineteenth to early twentieth centuries, an era that gave us enduring classics like *Peter and Wendy*, *Alice's Adventures in Wonderland*, *The Wonderful Wizard of Oz*, and *The Adventures of Tom Sawyer*. These stories are so deeply woven into our cultural fabric that they feel like they have always existed.

But the stories in this collection weren't chosen for their historical significance. I was looking for that unmistakable quality, something less tangible. That something that pulls us through time and space, stirring that recognizable sense of familiarity, even if it was my first read.

I chose stories that connect us and that leave an indelible mark across generations, transcending borders and time. I reached out to women from the United Kingdom, Canada, the United States, and Australia to share my selected recipes list. Just seeing the book names and foods stirred something in them, sparking memories and a longing to revisit the books. It was a beautiful reminder that whether we first met these stories in childhood or found them later, they continue to bring joy whenever we return to their pages.

This cookbook's collection of recipes serves as an additional bridge to your favorite worlds and to the past. Many recipes are served just as they might have been within the pages of our most loved books, whereas others are inspired interpretations, allowing a potential taste of your favorite characters' lives. But to truly connect with these dishes, I had to journey back in time.

Historical cookbooks were pored over, and I re-created dishes as they were originally made before adapting them for modern times or adding a literary twist. There's a common misconception that old recipes are stodgy or bland, but when the recipes are approached with curiosity, they reveal the mastery of the deft, skilled hands that would have once made them and that modern shortcuts often overlook. These recipes then become a way of preserving traditions passed down through generations. The ability to bake fresh bread, preserve fruits, and transform simple ingredients into something extraordinary—these are skills worth keeping alive.

Woven within these pages are recipes designed to involve the whole family and transform the kitchen into a hive of activity. Everyone can join in whisking together flour, eggs, milk, and butter into a Victorian sponge cake, ready to share, just like Sara shares with Becky in *A Little Princess*. Crisp vegetables and fresh herbs are blended, perfect for dipping and nibbling as we read along, following Peter Rabbit through Mr. McGregor's garden. And when the cooking is done, everyone will experience unmatched joy in biting into a hot, homemade crumpet laced with melting butter as if you were all out in the garden alongside Mary, Colin, and Dickon in *The Secret Garden*.

As you cook and bake your way through this collection of recipes and share these meals with friends and family, the stories behind them are bound to weave their own magic through every dish, offering new memories and taking you deeper into the beloved worlds that have shaped our imaginations.

10
Christmas Morning Buckwheat Pancakes
Little Women

13
Orange Marmalade Scrolls
Alice's Adventures in Wonderland

16
English Muffins Fit for a Princess
A Little Princess

19
Molasses Porridge
The Secret Garden

22
Banana Loaf
Just So Stories

24
Fried Egg Feast
The Adventures of Tom Sawyer

26
Dorothy's Soda Bread
The Wonderful Wizard of Oz

The Breakfast Table

But it was morning and, yes, it was a cherry-tree in full bloom outside of her window. With a bound she was out of bed and across the floor. She pushed up the sash—it went up stiffly and creakily, as if it hadn't been opened for a long time, which was the case; and it stuck so tight that nothing was needed to hold it up.

Anne dropped on her knees and gazed out into the June morning, her eyes glistening with delight. Oh, wasn't it beautiful? Wasn't it a lovely place?

—LUCY MAUD MONTGOMERY, *ANNE OF GREEN GABLES*

As the first light peeks through the curtains, so does the anticipation of the day ahead. For centuries, breakfast has been the most substantial meal of the day, providing the energy needed for both work and adventure.

In literature, a hearty breakfast is often the prelude to excitement—and what better way to prepare for the adventures of the day with your favorite characters, before you follow a White Rabbit into Wonderland with Alice or learn about the fantastical way an elephant's trunk became long, than with the tangy, creamy taste of Orange Marmalade Scrolls (page 13) or a slice of zesty Banana Loaf (page 22).

Begin your morning like Mary Lennox in *The Secret Garden*, with a steaming bowl of Molasses Porridge (page 19), rich with fresh cream and a drizzle of syrup—perfect for braving the bracing winds of a Yorkshire morning. Fuel your mischief with the sizzle of a Fried Egg Feast (page 24) in a pan just like Tom Sawyer and his friends or delight in the simple, satisfying comfort of a thick slice of warm soda bread (see page 26) before setting off down the Yellow Brick Road with Dorothy.

The recipes in this chapter also offer dishes for slow, chilly mornings that call for hot English Muffins Fit for a Princess (page 16), fresh off the griddle, to bring a warm comfort—just as they do for Sara in *A Little Princess*—and recipes for celebrations and holidays that call for special breakfasts—buckwheat pancakes (see page 10) from *Little Women* is teamed with special Christmas-flavored sides to capture the warmth of the season and celebrate the togetherness of family around the breakfast table.

MAKES EIGHT 4-INCH PANCAKES

Christmas Morning Buckwheat Pancakes

"Merry Christmas, little daughters! . . . Not far away from here lies a poor woman with a little newborn baby. Six children are huddled into one bed to keep from freezing, for they have no fire. There is nothing to eat over there, and the oldest boy came to tell me they were suffering hunger and cold. My girls, will you give them your breakfast as a Christmas present?" . . . Meg was already covering the buckwheats, and piling the bread into one big plate.

—LOUISA MAY ALCOTT, *LITTLE WOMEN*

On a frosty Christmas morning, the March sisters' festive feast transforms into a simple act of kindness. Adorning their breakfast table are buckwheat pancakes—"buckwheats" as they were commonly known in 1800s America. To capture the spirit of the March sisters and turn a simple meal into a special Christmas tradition, whip up a Yuletide butter infused with festive spices and serve with a spiced orange and cranberry compote.

YULETIDE BUTTER

½ cup unsalted butter, room temperature
¼ teaspoon sea salt
¼ teaspoon ground allspice
¼ teaspoon ground nutmeg
1 teaspoon ground cinnamon
¼ teaspoon almond extract
1 tablespoon light unsulphured molasses
2 tablespoons chopped candied orange peel (see page 106)

CHRISTMAS COMPOTE

2 cups frozen cranberries
2 cups granulated sugar
1 cup fresh orange juice
2 tablespoons orange zest
1 teaspoon ground cinnamon
8 whole cloves
2 whole star anise
1 teaspoon vanilla extract

BUCKWHEAT PANCAKES

1 cup buckwheat flour
1 teaspoon baking powder
½ teaspoon sea salt
1 cup whole milk
3 tablespoons raw sugar
1 large egg, room temperature
2 tablespoons melted unsalted butter
2 tablespoons vegetable oil, divided

TO MAKE THE YULETIDE BUTTER: In a small mixing bowl, combine the butter, sea salt, allspice, nutmeg, cinnamon, and almond extract. Mix until the spices are evenly distributed throughout the butter.

Stir in the molasses and candied orange peel, mixing well until all the ingredients are thoroughly combined.

Roll the butter in parchment paper to form a log. Chill in the refrigerator for 30 minutes to firm before serving. Yuletide butter can be stored in the refrigerator for up to 2 weeks.

TO MAKE THE CHRISTMAS COMPOTE: In a saucepan, heat the cranberries, granulated sugar, orange juice, orange zest, and cinnamon over medium heat. Stir to combine.

Place the cloves and star anise in a spice bag to keep the spices contained as the cranberries cook down to a mash; otherwise, finding the cloves will be impossible. Add to the saucepan.

Simmer, stirring occasionally, for 5 minutes. Reduce the heat to low and continue cooking until the sauce thickens, 15 minutes.

Remove the spice bag, stir in the vanilla, and let cool for about 5 minutes.

Ladle into clean 8-ounce jars. Leave the lid ajar and place in the refrigerator to set for 30 minutes before serving. Once set, close the lid and store in the refrigerator for up to 2 weeks.

Continued on page 12

CHEFS IN THE MAKING

AGES 3–5: Help count out the correct number of whole cloves and star anise.

AGES 10+: Take the lead and whip up the pancake batter from start to finish.

Be in charge of timing and flipping the pancakes—just keep an adult nearby the stove.

TO MAKE THE BUCKWHEAT PANCAKES: In a large, warmed bowl, sift together the buckwheat flour and baking powder using a fine-mesh strainer, then stir in the sea salt.

In a measuring cup, combine the whole milk and raw sugar. Microwave for 50 seconds on 100 percent power to warm, then stir to dissolve the sugar.

Whisk in the egg until combined, then add the melted butter. Whisk the milk mixture into the flour mixture to form a smooth batter.

In a 9-inch frying pan, heat the oil, swirling to coat, for 1 minute over medium heat.

Spoon in ¼ cup of batter and cook for 2 minutes, until bubbles form around the outside edge of the pancake and several appear in the middle. If you notice bubbles forming more on one side, rotate the pan halfway through to help evenly heat. The edges should look set, not be sloppy batter. Gently slide a spatula under the pancake to check that the underside is golden, then flip. Cook for another minute until the pancake has risen slightly in the center. To keep warm, place the cooked pancakes in the oven on a keep warm setting until all the batter is cooked.

Lower the heat to medium low and repeat with the remaining batter.

Serve with Christmas Compote and a pat of Yuletide Butter.

MAKES
12 SCROLLS

Orange Marmalade Scrolls

She took down a jar from one of the shelves as she passed: it was labelled "ORANGE MARMALADE," but to her great disappointment it was empty: she did not like to drop the jar, for fear of killing somebody underneath, so managed to put it into one of the cupboards as she fell past it.

—LEWIS CARROLL, *ALICE'S ADVENTURES IN WONDERLAND*

A White Rabbit pulling a watch out of its waistcoat pocket stirs Alice's curiosity, and the next moment she's following the creature and tumbling down a rabbit hole. There, Alice's fleeting encounter with an empty jar of orange marmalade marks the beginning of a topsy-turvy journey through Wonderland, introducing us to British Victorian customs and traditions, starting with this well-established breakfast condiment. This recipe turns the long-standing breakfast staple inside out, wrapping the tart flavor between layers of delicate, airy dough that no store-bought scroll can replicate.

DOUGH

½ cup boiling water
¾ cup whole milk
6 teaspoons raw sugar, divided
One 0.25-ounce packet active dry yeast
3½ cups all-purpose flour, divided, plus more for dusting
½ teaspoon sea salt
1 large egg, room temperature
1 tablespoon vegetable oil, plus more for greasing

FILLING

1 cup orange marmalade, divided

EGG WASH

1 large egg white, room temperature
1 tablespoon water, room temperature

FROSTING

4 ounces cream cheese, room temperature
2 tablespoons unsalted butter, room temperature
½ teaspoon vanilla extract
1 cup powdered sugar
2 tablespoons whole milk

TO MAKE THE DOUGH: In a small bowl, stir together the boiling water and whole milk. Add 2 teaspoons of raw sugar and the yeast and stir to combine.

Add ½ cup of all-purpose flour and stir with a fork to form a smooth batter. Set aside in a warm spot for 15 minutes. If your kitchen is cold, preheat your oven to 100°F, then turn it off before placing the bowl inside to help the batter rise. The batter will expand during the 15 minutes.

Pour some hot water (around 110°F) into the bowl of a stand mixer, or a large mixing bowl if you're using a hand mixer. Swirl the water around to warm the bowl to bring your equipment to a similar temperature as the dough. Drain and dry with a clean kitchen towel.

Add the remaining 3 cups of all-purpose flour, sea salt, and the remaining 4 teaspoons of raw sugar to the bowl. Stir to combine.

Tip: When measuring flour, pour the flour into the measuring cup instead of scooping directly into the bag of flour. Scooping will compact the flour, resulting in more flour than needed, leading to a dense and dry dough.

Make a well in the middle of the flour mixture. Add the egg, the batter mixture, and the oil. Mix the dough at low speed until it begins to come together.

TO KNEAD THE DOUGH IN A STAND MIXER: Switch to a dough hook attachment and knead for 10 minutes until the dough is smooth and elastic. The dough should pull away from the edges of the bowl.

Every few minutes, turn off the mixer to pull the dough off the attachment back into the bowl. Temporarily transfer the dough from the bowl onto a large plate as you grease the inside of the bowl.

Continued on page 15

CHEFS IN THE MAKING

AGES 3–5: Swirl marmalade over the rolled-out dough with a spatula.

Dollop frosting on top.

AGES 5–10: Ask an adult to watch over as you measure and mix the frosting ingredients.

AGES 10+: There are several parts to this recipe. Take charge of the whole recipe—dough, filling, frosting, and all.

FACT NOT FICTION

When Lewis Carroll penned Alice's Adventures in Wonderland *in the late 1800s, marmalade had already become a staple of the Victorian English breakfast to serve with toast. Oranges were recorded as being imported from Spain and Portugal into Britain in the fifteenth and sixteenth centuries. However, Seville oranges are too bitter to eat raw, so they were transformed into a spreadable preserve. Over time, Seville oranges became so closely associated with marmalade that they are now considered the traditional and "correct" fruit for making this beloved breakfast spread.*

TO KNEAD THE DOUGH BY HAND: When mixing dough by hand, a wooden spoon may be needed for the final stages of combining as the dough thickens.

Turn the dough out onto a lightly floured kitchen counter and knead by hand for 10 minutes, using the palms of your hands to stretch and fold it until the surface is smooth and elastic.

Use about 2 teaspoons of vegetable oil to grease the large mixing bowl. Place the dough back into the bowl and cover with a clean, damp kitchen towel. Place in a warm spot to rise for 1 hour.

Dust your clean kitchen counter lightly with flour. Roll out the dough in to a 12-by-18-inch rectangle.

TO FILL: Spread ½ cup of marmalade thickly and evenly to all the edges of the dough.

Roll the dough from the long edge, then use a bread knife to slice it into 1½-inch-thick scrolls.

Butter a 10-by-12-inch roasting pan. Place the dough in the pan, scroll side up, leaving ½-inch gap between each piece.

TO MAKE THE EGG WASH: In a small bowl, whisk together the egg white and water with a fork. Brush over the scrolls.

Cover with a clean, damp kitchen tea towel and set aside to proof for 30 minutes, allowing the dough to rise again after being rolled and shaped.

Preheat the oven to 350°F.

Remove the towel and bake the scrolls for 25 minutes, until the tops of the scrolls have just a hint of golden color and are firm but spring back slightly when gently pressed. Remove from the oven and let cool while you make the frosting.

TO MAKE THE FROSTING: In the bowl of a stand mixer, or a large mixing bowl if using a hand mixer, beat the cream cheese and butter together until smooth.

Add the vanilla and continue to beat until fully incorporated.

With the mixer on low speed, gradually add the powdered sugar. Once all is incorporated, increase the speed to medium and beat until smooth. Pour in the whole milk and mix until the mixture is smooth.

Spoon the frosting evenly over the scrolls and place 2 teaspoons of marmalade on top of each before serving.

Frosted scrolls can be stored in an airtight container in the refrigerator for 3 days. To serve, place them in the microwave for 10 seconds on 100 percent power to soften. Unfrosted scrolls freeze well in an airtight container for up to 3 months.

MAKES
8 MUFFINS

English Muffins Fit for a Princess

Imagine, if you can, what the rest of the evening was like. How they crouched by the fire which blazed and leaped and made so much of itself in the little grate. How they removed the covers of the dishes, and found rich, hot, savory soup, which was a meal in itself, and sandwiches and toast and muffins enough for both of them. The mug from the washstand was used as Becky's tea cup, and the tea was so delicious that it was not necessary to pretend that it was anything but tea.

—FRANCES HODGSON BURNETT, *A LITTLE PRINCESS*

Sara Crewe was raised in comfort, but when her father's death leaves her penniless, she is reduced to a life of hardship, working as a servant in the very boarding house where she was once a favored student. Cold, hungry, and exhausted, she endures with quiet dignity, but her struggles do not go unnoticed. Her dismal, cold attic transforms like magic in the middle of the night into a warm and comfortable space, filled with delicious and nourishing foods, thanks to the thoughtful and nimble action of Ram Dass, the servant from next door. The muffins mentioned in this story are found in many classic English stories. Far from the sweet, cupcake-like treats many know, they are made from a soft, yeasty dough in round shapes. More in line with bread, they are cooked on the stove rather than the oven, ready for a princess's tea or a cozy evening by the fire.

INGREDIENTS

1 cup warm water, divided
½ teaspoon raw sugar
One 0.25-ounce packet active dry yeast
3 cups all-purpose flour
1 teaspoon sea salt
2 tablespoons vegetable oil
¾ cup warm whole milk
Olive oil, for greasing
1½ cups semolina or rice flour
Unsalted butter, for serving

In a small bowl, combine ¼ cup of warm water, the raw sugar, and yeast. Let sit for 15 minutes until frothy.

Pour the all-purpose flour into a large microwave-friendly bowl.

Tip: When measuring, pour the flour into a measuring cup instead of scooping directly into the bag of flour. Scooping will compact the flour, resulting in more flour than needed, leading to a dense dough.

Warm the all-purpose flour in the microwave for 30 seconds on 100 percent power. Mix in the sea salt and make a well in the middle of the flour.

Stir the vegetable oil, remaining ¾ cup of warm water, and warm milk into the yeast mixture, then pour into the warm flour.

Stir for 2 minutes until the dough is smooth. The dough will be sticky and will not form a ball or be kneadable.

Lightly oil the dough surface with 1 teaspoon of olive oil. Cover with a clean kitchen towel or plate and let rise for 50 minutes in a warm spot.

In a microwave-friendly bowl, warm the semolina flour in the microwave for 30 seconds on 100 percent power to use for dusting.

Pour 1 cup of warm semolina flour onto a sheet pan for resting the dough and set aside the remaining ½ cup for dusting your hands as you handle the dough.

Punch down the risen dough, then divide it into eight pieces, handling and compressing the dough as little as possible. Gently shape the pieces into rounds, like slightly flattened buns, on the floured pan.

Let rest for 30 minutes, covered with a kitchen towel.

Continued on page 18

Heat a large griddle or cast-iron pan over medium-low heat. Using the semolina flour from the floured tray, sprinkle 1 to 2 tablespoons on the pan to monitor hot spots.

Gently transfer the English muffins to the pan and cook for 10 minutes, twisting the pan occasionally to manage the heat. Use the semolina flour as your visual guide. When it darkens to a golden color, lift one muffin with a spatula to see if the bottom is evenly golden brown, adjusting the pan as needed. Flip the muffins and cook for another 10 minutes, until the second side is also golden brown. Replace the semolina flour before cooking the next batch of English muffins.

Store in an airtight container at room temperature for up to 2 days. The traditional way to toast English muffins is to reheat them whole. Using the pan on the stove, reheat both sides before tearing open and buttering generously.

NOTE: Managing heat while cooking quick breads—whether it's the Garden Crumpets (page 35) or these English muffins—can be tricky. The semolina isn't just to prevent sticking. It also helps you monitor for hot spots. If the flour on the pan begins to brown too quickly, lower the heat. If the flour darkens too much, remove the pan from the heat and let it cool before continuing. Consider using a trivet for gas stoves or a heat diffuser on an electric stove for better heat control.

CHEFS IN THE MAKING

AGES 3–5: Pour the warm semolina onto a sheet pan to make a cozy bed for the dough to rest.

AGES 5–10: Drizzle on the olive oil and help cover the bowl to keep the dough soft as it rises.

AGES 10+: Take the lead on the full recipe—from mixing to shaping and rising.

Stovetop cooking takes focus: Keep an eye on those golden bottoms and ask for backup from an adult adjusting the heat if needed.

FACT NOT FICTION

English muffins were traditionally shaped by hand and cooked on a griddle, giving them a charmingly rustic, uneven appearance. The invention of metal rings allowed for the uniform shape we recognize today. This recipe follows the old-fashioned method of hand-shaping and rising in warmed flour, but crumpet rings can be used for more perfectly circular shapes.

Molasses Porridge

A table in the center was set with a good substantial breakfast. But she had always had a very small appetite, and she looked with something more than indifference at the first plate Martha set before her.

"I don't want it," she said.

"Tha' doesn't want thy porridge!" Martha exclaimed incredulously.

"No."

"Tha' doesn't know how good it is. Put a bit o' treacle on it or a bit o' sugar."

—FRANCES HODGSON BURNETT, *THE SECRET GARDEN*

Accustomed to a life of being waited on in British colonial India, Mary Lennox arrives at Misselthwaite Manor—a sprawling estate in Northern England—after the sudden death of her parents. Disagreeable and unprepared for even the simplest tasks like dressing herself, she initially scoffs at the plain, hearty foods of her new home. Mary might initially be indifferent to a dish of hot oatmeal porridge, but with enough time she'll find the fresh Yorkshire air and the mystery of a long-forgotten locked garden soon awaken both her curiosity and her appetite. To top off a steaming bowl of traditional oatmeal porridge, a drizzle of heavy cream followed by a spoonful of golden syrup or light treacle have been a classic choice for centuries for a reason and is still the recommended combination here. To fill out the breakfast table, serve with a side of spiced poached pears.

POACHED PEARS

2 cups water
1 cup raw sugar
3 cardamom pods
1 whole star anise
5 black peppercorns
2 pears, cored and quartered

PORRIDGE

1 cup steel-cut oats
3 cups boiling water
¼ teaspoon sea salt
¾ cup heavy cream
¼ cup unsulphured molasses or light treacle

TO MAKE THE POACHED PEARS: In a medium saucepan, combine the water, raw sugar, cardamom pods, star anise, and black peppercorns.

Bring the mixture to a simmer over medium-low heat for 5 minutes, stirring occasionally to dissolve the sugar.

Add the quartered pears to the saucepan. If the pears float above the surface, use a smaller lid to hold them down under the syrup.

Cover with a fitted lid and cook for about 25 minutes, until the pears are tender but still intact.

Serve the poached pears and syrup in a bowl on the side.

Continued on page 21

CHEFS IN THE MAKING

AGES 3–5: Count out the cardamom pods, star anise, and black peppercorns.

Drizzle premeasured cream or molasses over the finished porridge.

AGES 10+: Porridge is one of the most satisfying breakfasts to master. Try making it yourself with adult supervision when using the stove.

TO MAKE THE PORRIDGE: In a medium saucepan, combine the steel-cut oats, boiling water, and sea salt.

Place the saucepan over medium-low heat and cook for 5 minutes to bring to a boil.

Reduce the heat to low and continue cooking for about 20 minutes, stirring occasionally, until the oats are tender and creamy.

To serve, divide the oats into four bowls.

Top each serving with a splash of heavy cream and a tablespoon of molasses.

MAKES
1 LOAF

Banana Loaf

That very next morning, when there was nothing left of the Equinoxes, because the Precession had preceded according to precedent, this 'satiable Elephant's Child took a hundred pounds of bananas (the little short red kind), and a hundred pounds of sugar-cane (the long purple kind), and seventeen melons (the greeny-crackly kind), and said to all his dear families, "Goodbye. I am going to the great grey-green, greasy Limpopo River, all set about with fever-trees, to find out what the Crocodile has for dinner."

—RUDYARD KIPLING, *JUST SO STORIES*

Just So Stories is a collection of whimsical origin tales that explain how animals came to have their distinctive features—like how the leopard got its spots or how the elephant got its trunk. In "The Elephant's Child," a young, curious elephant, born with only a short, bulgy nose, sets off to discover what crocodiles eat for dinner. His insatiable curiosity leads him to the "great grey-green, greasy Limpopo River," where a tug-of-war with a cunning crocodile stretches his nose into the trunk we recognize today. No longer needing to wait for bananas to fall, this new trunk proves immensely useful, as he can now pluck them straight from the tree. Inspired by all the bananas he can now pick, this loaf transforms overripe bananas into a snack—delicious out of the oven but even better when toasted and topped with butter.

INGREDIENTS

1½ cups mashed overripe banana (see note)
2 large eggs, room temperature
½ cup raw sugar
1 teaspoon vanilla extract
Zest of 1 large navel orange
2 cups all-purpose flour
1 tablespoon baking powder
¼ teaspoon ground nutmeg
½ teaspoon ground cinnamon
½ teaspoon sea salt

Preheat the oven to 425°F. Line a 10-inch loaf pan with parchment paper.

In a large mixing bowl, combine the banana, eggs, raw sugar, vanilla, and orange zest.

In another large mixing bowl, sift together the flour, baking powder, nutmeg, cinnamon, and sea salt. Gently fold the dry ingredients into the wet mixture until just combined, being careful not to overmix. Pour the batter into the prepared loaf pan.

Lower the oven temperature to 400°F and bake for 40 minutes, until a skewer inserted into the center of the loaf comes out clean.

Allow the loaf to cool in the pan for 10 minutes before transferring to a wire rack to cool completely. Cut into 1-inch slices to serve or place in an airtight container at room temperature and store for up to 3 days.

NOTE: Banana bread is a classic way to use up overripe bananas, but what if your bananas are neither ripe nor overripe? Preheat the oven to 325°F, place the unpeeled bananas on a baking sheet, and bake for 10 minutes, flipping halfway through. Once the skins have darkened, remove from the oven, let cool, then peel to use.

CHEFS IN THE MAKING

AGES 3–5: Squish bananas with a potato masher.

Shake and sift the flour and spices through a fine-mesh strainer, then use a big spoon to mix everything together.

AGES 5–10: Crack eggs into a separate bowl and make it a habit to check for shells. Learn to zest oranges with a fine grater.

AGES 10+: Confident bakers can handle every step, with a little supervision around the oven if needed.

Fried Egg Feast

After dinner all the gang turned out to hunt for turtle eggs on the bar. They went about poking sticks into the sand, and when they found a soft place they went down on their knees and dug with their hands. Sometimes they would take fifty or sixty eggs out of one hole. They were perfectly round white things a trifle smaller than an English walnut. They had a famous fried-egg feast that night, and another on Friday morning.

—MARK TWAIN, *THE ADVENTURES OF TOM SAWYER*

The image of Tom Sawyer and his companions feasting on fried eggs by campfire brings outdoor adventures along the Mississippi to life, capturing one of the many experiences this clever, mischievous orphan has with his friends. To replicate the rich, smoky flavor of a campfire-cooked meal in a more conventional kitchen setting, opt for triple-smoked bacon with plenty of fat. Lay the bacon on a wire rack set on a sheet pan, not only to crisp the bacon evenly on both sides but to capture the drippings in the pan below to use for frying the eggs. Though this won't replicate the flavors of a campfire, it brings a hint of outdoor cooking indoors and recalls Tom's adventures.

INGREDIENTS

12 slices hickory smoked thick-cut bacon

¼ teaspoon gluten-free liquid smoke

8 large eggs

1 teaspoon sea salt

1 teaspoon ground black pepper

CHEFS IN THE MAKING

AGES 5–10: Lay out bacon strips neatly on a wire rack.

Crack eggs straight into the pan with a steady hand. Just be sure an adult is nearby to help if needed.

AGES 10+: Take the lead on oven-baking bacon and draining off drippings safely.

Gentle, steady heat is the secret to perfect eggs.

Preheat the oven to 400°F.

Arrange the bacon slices on a wire rack set over a sheet pan to catch the drippings. Bake for 20 minutes, until the bacon is crispy and browned.

In a 9-inch frying pan, combine 2 tablespoons of the bacon fat drippings with the liquid smoke. Heat the pan over low heat for 1 minute. Crack in eight eggs and cook on low heat until the egg whites are translucent, about 5 minutes. Sprinkle sea salt and pepper evenly on top.

Serve two eggs with three slices of bacon per person.

PAIRS WELL WITH: To fill out the meal, serve the bacon and eggs with Corn Dodgers (page 80) from *The Adventures of Huckleberry Finn.*

MAKES
1 LOAF

Dorothy's Soda Bread

She took a little basket and filled it with bread from the cupboard, laying a white cloth over the top. Then she looked down at her feet and noticed how old and worn her shoes were.

"They surely will never do for a long journey, Toto," she said.

—L. FRANK BAUM, *THE WONDERFUL WIZARD OF OZ*

Dorothy, a Kansas farm girl, and her pet dog, Toto, find themselves swept away by a cyclone to the magical Land of Oz. Before setting off down the Yellow Brick Road to the Emerald City, she packs a simple basket of bread for her journey ahead. There's something wonderful about being able to bake your own fresh bread, and soda bread, with its quick rise, is the perfect choice—ready in no time for whatever adventures are to come.

INGREDIENTS

2 cups whole wheat flour, plus more for dusting

Tip: The simplicity of this recipe means the flavor of the whole wheat flour is key. For the best taste, use a fresh bag rather than one that has been sitting in your cupboard, as whole wheat flour spoils more quickly than white flour. This is because it contains the entire grain, including the bran and germ, which are rich in natural oils that can turn rancid over time.

1 tablespoon baking powder
½ teaspoon sea salt
1 cup whole milk
Butter, for greasing

Preheat the oven to 425°F.

In a large bowl, sift together the whole wheat flour, baking powder, and sea salt. Pour the whole milk into the dry ingredients, stirring until just combined, forming a sticky dough.

Coat your hands generously with flour. Gently knead the dough to shape it into a round loaf about 6 inches in diameter.

Butter and flour a baking sheet and place the shaped dough on it. Bake for 20 minutes, until the loaf has a golden, crusty top. It's natural for soda and quick breads to develop a natural split in the top as the dough expands quickly in the hot oven. This seam will look crusted over.

Let the bread cool completely before slicing to serve.

NOTE: Soda bread has a shorter shelf life than yeast-based bread and is best eaten on the same day, which is why this recipe makes a small batch. Wrap in a clean kitchen towel at room temperature to store. Bread can be rewarmed or toasted over the following 2 days.

CHEFS IN THE MAKING

AGES 3–5: This dough is sticky, so cover little hands in flour to help gently knead the bread.

AGES 5–10: Have an adult guide you through each step, but you can measure, sift, mix, and shape this bread yourself. Have an adult help you place the bread in the hot oven.

AGES 10+: This is a great recipe to build confidence with quick breads. Take charge of the whole process, from mixing and shaping the dough to baking it in the oven. Just be sure to ask for supervision when handling the hot tray.

FACT NOT FICTION

Soda bread became popular in the mid-1800s with the introduction of chemical leavening agents like baking soda (also known as bicarbonate of soda in the United Kingdom), which changed baking worldwide by eliminating the need for yeast and lengthy proofing times. An acid is essential for baking soda to activate, which is why you'll always see buttermilk, vinegar, or lemon juice in old traditional recipes. Today, baking powder combines baking soda, a powdered acid, and a stabilizer like rice flour, which means only water is needed to activate it, with the heat creating the final rise. The result is a dense, hearty bread that is both satisfying and quick to prepare—perfect for last-minute baking.

33
Wendy's Mammee-Apple Slice
Peter and Wendy

35
Garden Crumpets
The Secret Garden

38
Benjamin Bunny's Mini Caramelized Onion Quiches
The Tale of Benjamin Bunny

41
Currant Buns
A Little Princess

44
Winnie-the-Pooh's Sticky Honey Cakes
Winnie-the-Pooh

46
Coconut Pineapple Petit Fours
The Story of Doctor Dolittle

49
Crab-Apple Preserve
Anne of Green Gables

Morning and Afternoon Tea

"Nearly eleven o'clock," said Pooh happily. "You're just in time for a little smackerel of something."

—A.A. MILNE, *THE HOUSE AT POOH CORNER*

Winnie-the-Pooh famously "liked a little something at eleven o'clock in the morning," and he's not alone in appreciating a midmorning snack. Morning tea—or elevenses, as it's also called in British literature—is a little pause between breakfast and lunch for a pot of tea and small bites such as cookies (or biscuits as they're known in the United Kingdom), like *A Little Princess*'s Currant Buns (page 41)—just enough to tide you over until lunch.

Afternoon tea, on the other hand, varied depending on circumstance. Though modest bread-and-butter was common among the working class, I suggest dressing up your midmorning snack with *Anne of Green Gables*' Crab-Apple Preserve (page 49) to create a special treat! Sharing afternoon tea with friends and family is a perfect reason to enjoy a variety of sweet and savory delights, such as staples like the Garden Crumpets (page 35), alongside sweet little Coconut Pineapple Petit Fours (page 46) inspired by *The Story of Doctor Dolittle*, or Benjamin Bunny's Mini Caramelized Onion Quiches (page 38) for a savory bite.

And for those wishing to capture the fantastical experience of the Mad Hatter's Tea Party from *Alice's Adventures in Wonderland*, which was written to make fun of Victorian afternoon tea rituals, pair the dishes in this chapter with recipes for Alice's famous encounter with a magical bottle and cakes (see pages 117 and 119), to add a touch of magic to your afternoon tea.

MAKES
16 SQUARES

Wendy's Mammee-Apple Slice

Their chief food was roasted bread-fruit, yams, coconuts, baked pig, mammee-apples, tappa rolls and bananas, washed down with calabashes of poe-poe; but you never exactly knew whether there would be a real meal or just a make-believe, it all depended upon Peter's whim.

—J. M. BARRIE, *PETER AND WENDY*

Wendy Darling and her brothers are whisked away to Neverland by Peter Pan, a boy who never grows up. In this magical world of mermaids, fairies, and pirates, Peter and the Lost Boys—children who, like him, never age—live in a world where even mealtimes blur the line between fantasy and feast. For those who've grown up beyond the tropics, visions of the Lost Boys gorging on mammee apples and coconuts and sipping out of drinking containers made of dried gourds offer our imagination glimpses of an unknown world. Just like Peter Pan, imagination is one essential ingredient required to transform familiar fruits of apricots, passion fruit, and raspberry into something capturing the essence of the mammee apple. A dusting of citric acid brings the tang, so all you'll have to do is slice in and let your imagination take flight and bring you closer to Neverland.

FILLING

½ cup chopped dried apricots
¾ cup apricot jam
1 cup frozen raspberries
¾ cup passion fruit purée
Granulated sugar and water
2 tablespoons fresh lime juice
1 teaspoon citric acid

CRUMB

1¼ cups all-purpose flour
¼ teaspoon baking soda
¾ cup old-fashioned rolled oats
¾ cup desiccated coconut
1 cup lightly packed light brown sugar
¼ teaspoon sea salt
¾ cup cold unsalted butter, cut into ½-inch cubes

SERVING

4 cups vanilla ice cream

Preheat the oven to 375°F.

TO MAKE THE FILLING*:* In a medium saucepan over medium heat, combine the dried apricots, apricot jam, raspberries, passion fruit purée, and lime juice.

Cook for 5 minutes to bring the mixture to a boil.

Continue cooking for an additional 5 minutes, stirring occasionally, until the mixture has thickened and looks glossy. The raspberries will have broken down, and the apricot pieces will have softened but will still hold their shape.

Turn off the heat and stir in the citric acid.

TO MAKE THE CRUMB*:* In the bowl of a stand mixer, or a large mixing bowl if using a hand mixer, sift together the flour and baking soda.

Using the paddle attachment, stir in the oats, coconut, brown sugar, and sea salt.

Add the cold butter cubes and mix for about 2 minutes, until the butter is incorporated into the dry ingredients, forming a coarse, moist crumb.

TO ASSEMBLE*:* Grease a 9-inch-square baking pan and line it with parchment paper.

Pour half of the crumb mixture into the pan and press down firmly. Spread the filling evenly over the crumb layer.

Cover the filling with the remaining crumb mixture and pat down gently.

Bake for 40 minutes until the top is golden brown.

Continued on page 34

CHEFS IN THE MAKING

AGES 3–5: Press the crumb mixture into the pan with clean hands.

Help sprinkle the top layer of crumbs and pat down.

AGES 5–10: Help an adult by measuring and mixing together the crumb mixture with the stand mixer.

For the slice to not stick to the pan, the pan needs to be lined. Help get the butter across the whole surface of the baking pan and into the corners so the parchment paper doesn't slide around.

AGES 10+: Try assembling the slice yourself, with supervision when using the stove and oven.

TO SERVE: Allow the bars to cool for 1 hour before cutting into 16 squares and serving each slice with a scoop of ice cream.

Store in an airtight container in the refrigerator for up to 1 week.

PAIRS WELL WITH: Create an entire Peter and Wendy–inspired meal and pair this slice with Tappa Rolls (page 70).

MAKES SIX 4-INCH CRUMPETS

Garden Crumpets

It was an agreeable idea, easily carried out, and when the white cloth was spread upon the grass, with hot tea and buttered toast and crumpets, a delightfully hungry meal was eaten, and several birds on domestic errands paused to inquire what was going on and were led into investigating crumbs with great activity. Nut and Shell whisked up trees with pieces of cake and Soot took the entire half of a buttered crumpet into a corner and pecked at and examined and turned it over and made hoarse remarks about it until he decided to swallow it all joyfully in one gulp.

—FRANCES HODGSON BURNETT, *THE SECRET GARDEN*

Within the high walls of a hidden garden, spring has awakened with plum, cherry, and apple trees blossoming in shades of pink and white. It's a perfect setting for Colin's first chance to explore this enchanted space. Long confined to his room at Misselthwaite Manor, he's accompanied by his cousin, Mary Lennox, who has been equally spoiled from her childhood, and Dickon, a local boy with an innate connection to nature. As the day unwinds and the fresh air brings about an appetite, a basket for afternoon tea is brought out. The contents of which—a stack of buttered crumpets—stir curiosity and delight among a feathered companion, a joy likely to be mirrored by anyone who tries their hand at making these at home. Whether enjoyed outdoors or indoors, each bite will serve as a reminder of simple pleasures, whisking you away to the hidden corners of an English garden.

INGREDIENTS

¾ cup plus 2 tablespoons warm water, divided
¼ teaspoon granulated sugar
½ teaspoon active dry yeast
1 cup (150 grams or 5.5 ounces) all-purpose flour
½ teaspoon sea salt
½ teaspoon baking powder
6 teaspoons vegetable oil, divided
Unsalted butter, for serving

SPECIAL EQUIPMENT

Scale
Handheld whisk or electric hand mixer
Six 4-inch crumpet rings
Square griddle (optional)
Stove (see note)

In a small bowl or measuring cup, mix together ½ cup warm water and the granulated sugar before stirring in active dry yeast. Set aside for 15 minutes until the yeast begins to foam.

Pour the flour into a medium microwave-friendly bowl. Microwave the flour for 15 seconds at 100 percent power to warm it. Stir in the sea salt, then whisk in ¼ cup of warm water. Add in the yeast mixture, whisking as you pour.

Tip: If not using a scale, pour the flour into a measuring cup to keep the flour from compacting. This loose flour should equal the right amount. Note that scooping it with a measuring cup will compact the flour and you'll end up with too much flour, up to ¼ to ⅓ of a cup more, and a dough rather than a batter will form.

In a small bowl or measuring cup, use a fork to whisk the baking powder into 2 tablespoons of warm water before adding it to the flour mixture. Use a handheld whisk or electric hand mixer set to medium to medium-high speed to whisk it together vigorously, about 1 minute.

Cover the batter with cling wrap or beeswax food wrap and set it in a warm spot for 1 hour. Oil and flour the crumpet rings and set aside.

Place a square griddle or medium-sized frying pan over medium heat. If using, add a stove trivet to help manage the heat. Heat the frying pan or griddle for 1 minute, then pour in 1 teaspoon vegetable oil per crumpet and heat for 1 minute more.

Continued on page 36

Place the crumpet rings in the frying pan or griddle. The oil is hot enough when the flour on the crumpet rings sizzles. Pour in ¼ cup of batter and cook 1 minute, then reduce the heat to low and cook 4 minutes further, until bubbles form and pop along the entire crumpet surface and the batter looks set but pale.

Use tongs to remove the rings, leaving behind the crumpets, and flip the crumpets, cooking them for 30 seconds, until they turn lightly golden. Remove from the pan and cover with a kitchen towel to keep them warm as you finish cooking remaining crumpets. Serve them immediately with butter.

Crumpets can be stored in an airtight container at room temperature and toasted to reheat the next day.

NOTE: Using a stove trivet helps manage heat and avoids burnt crumpets. Crumpets need higher heat in order for the bubbles to form properly, but this can also easily burn crumpets. A trivet helps circulate the stove's heat more evenly.

PAIRS WELL WITH: Serve these crumpets alongside hot tea, buttered toast, and the Seed Cake (page 57) found in the Picnics and Light Luncheons chapter to re-create your own secret garden experience.

CHEFS IN THE MAKING

AGES 5–10: Help pour the batter into the crumpet rings with supervision.

When the crumpets are cooking on the stove, sometimes the air bubbles that form don't pop. With supervision, help pop them with a wooden skewer.

FACT NOT FICTION

Like their cousins, the English muffin and the pancake, crumpets are made on the stove. What distinguishes crumpets is their yeast and baking powder batter, creating a spongy texture riddled with holes on the surface, perfect for capturing pools of melted butter or jam. Though Victorian innovation brought crumpet rings, providing a uniform shape and height, they can be made without these molds, maintaining their traditional charm.

English
TEA

MAKES 12 MINI QUICHES

Benjamin Bunny's Mini Caramelized Onion Quiches

Little Benjamin took one look, and then, in half a minute less than no time, he hid himself and Peter and the onions underneath a large basket . . .

—BEATRIX POTTER, *THE TALE OF BENJAMIN BUNNY*

Mischief unfolds once again for Peter Rabbit, this time with his cousin Benjamin Bunny. With Mr. and Mrs. McGregor out for the day, the bunnies embark on a mission to retrieve Peter's clothes that are being used on a scarecrow and to gather onions for Peter's mother along the way. However, their adventure takes a turn when they find themselves trapped under a basket guarded by a cat. Caramelizing onions on the stove transform tear-inducing raw onions, coaxing out their natural sweetness and richness. This savory jam shines as the key ingredient of these mini quiches but also makes a tasty addition to a cheese platter. Served hot or cold, these bite-size quiches are perfect for on-the-go lunches next to a fresh garden salad.

SHORTCRUST PASTRY

1¼ cups all-purpose flour, plus more for kneading
½ teaspoon sea salt
7 tablespoons cold unsalted butter, cut into ¾-inch cubes
2 tablespoons cold water

CARAMELIZED ONION JAM

3 tablespoons olive oil
3 medium yellow onions, peeled and finely cut into ⅛-inch-thick slices
½ teaspoon sea salt
2 tablespoons balsamic vinegar
2 tablespoons lightly packed light brown sugar
¼ teaspoon ground white pepper

QUICHE

2 large eggs, room temperature
¼ cup ricotta cheese
¼ cup whole milk
¼ teaspoon sea salt
¼ teaspoon ground white pepper
1 garlic clove, minced
1 cup grated cheddar cheese
⅓ cup Caramelized Onion Jam

SPECIAL EQUIPMENT

4-inch pastry ring

TO MAKE THE PASTRY IN A FOOD PROCESSOR: In a food processor, combine the flour and sea salt. Turn on the processor and add the cold butter cubes. Pulse for 10 seconds until the flour and butter combine into a wet crumb.

With the processor running, pour the cold water in a steady stream through the tube feeder until the dough forms into a ball.

TO MAKE THE PASTRY BY HAND: In a large bowl, combine the flour and sea salt.

Add the butter to the flour mixture and use two forks or your fingertips to work the butter into the flour until the mixture resembles coarse crumbs.

Add the cold water gradually, stirring with a fork until the dough begins to come together.

Once the dough forms a ball, turn it out onto a lightly floured kitchen counter and gently knead it a couple of times to bring it together.

Wrap the dough in parchment paper and place it in the refrigerator for 1 hour while you make the caramelized onion jam and filling.

Continued on page 40

SEEDS

CHEFS IN THE MAKING

AGES 3–5: Get creative with cookie cutters or a pastry ring to stamp out dough circles.

AGES 5–10: Ready to dive into a big list of ingredients? Be a helper by reading them out loud to make sure everything's in place.

TO MAKE THE CARAMELIZED ONION JAM: In a 9-inch heavy-bottomed frying pan over low heat, heat the olive oil for 1 minute.

Add the onions to the pan, sprinkle with the sea salt, and stir to coat with the olive oil. Cover the pan with a lid and cook for 20 minutes, stirring every 2 to 3 minutes.

Add the balsamic vinegar, brown sugar, and white pepper. Stir to combine. Cook for an additional 10 minutes, stirring every 2 to 3 minutes to avoid burning, until the mixture forms a jam-like consistency.

Remove from the heat and set aside to cool. The mixture will reduce to ⅓ cup.

TO MAKE THE QUICHE: Preheat the oven to 350°F.

In a large mixing bowl, whisk together the eggs, ricotta, milk, sea salt, white pepper, and minced garlic until well combined. Fold in the cheddar cheese and caramelized onion jam.

On a lightly floured surface, roll out the dough and use a 4-inch pastry ring to cut twelve circles to fit into a standard muffin tin. Butter and lightly flour each muffin cavity, then press a dough circle into each. Spoon a heaping tablespoon of the egg mixture into each tin.

Bake for 25 minutes or until the filling is set and the tops are golden brown.

Allow to cool slightly in the tin before serving warm. To store, cool completely, then place in an airtight container in the refrigerator for up to 3 days.

MAKES 20 BUNS

Currant Buns

And it was a baker's shop, and a cheerful, stout, motherly woman with rosy cheeks was putting into the window a tray of delicious newly baked hot buns, fresh from the oven—large, plump, shiny buns, with currants in them.

—FRANCES HODGSON BURNETT, *A LITTLE PRINCESS*

Sara Crewe experiences a very different life from the one she is accustomed to. Orphaned and penniless, she's forced to work as a servant in the very boardinghouse where she was once a student. Despite her gnawing hunger, Sara's upbringing prompts her to give away five of the six buns she purchases with a found fourpence to a hungry street child. Her act of selfless kindness does not go unnoticed; the baker woman, moved by Sara's gesture, extends a similar kindness to the hungry street child, showing how our small deeds can create a ripple of goodwill, many times without our knowledge. Served warm and fresh out of the oven, currant buns are a delicious way to offer an old-fashioned taste of the past, when yeast was the common way to rise breads and cakes, to share with others during a cozy afternoon tea.

CURRANT BUNS

1¼ cups whole milk, divided
¼ cup raw sugar, divided
2 teaspoons active dry yeast
¼ cup unsalted butter, room temperature
1 large egg, room temperature
⅓ cup currants
4 cups all-purpose flour
½ teaspoon sea salt

ICING GLAZE

1 cup powdered sugar
3 tablespoons 2 percent milk

TO MAKE THE CURRANT BUNS: In a glass measuring cup, warm ¼ cup of whole milk in the microwave at 100 percent power for 30 seconds. The milk will be warm to the touch but not scalding hot.

Stir in ½ teaspoon of sugar and the active dry yeast and set aside for 10 minutes to foam.

In a medium microwave-friendly mixing bowl, warm the remaining 1 cup of whole milk and the butter in the microwave at 100 percent power for 1 minute. Use a fork to whisk in the remaining sugar and the egg until combined.

In a large microwave-safe mixing bowl, heat the currants in the microwave at 100 percent power for 20 seconds.

Stir in the flour and sea salt to combine, then stir in both milk mixtures until a dough is formed. Cover with a clean kitchen towel and place in a warm spot for 1 hour to rise.

Line two baking sheets with parchment paper. Preheat the oven to 375°F. Position an oven rack to the middle position.

Split the dough into 20 small buns and place them on the baking sheets. Cover with kitchen towels and let rise for 20 minutes.

Bake for 15 minutes until golden brown. Remove and let cool for 10 minutes.

TO MAKE THE ICING GLAZE: In a small bowl, mix the powdered sugar and 2 percent milk with a fork until smooth and drizzle over each bun with a spoon. Allow to dry for 15 minutes, then serve.

Currant buns can be stored in an airtight container at room temperature for 3 days.

fig. 1
A LITTLE PRINCESS

CHEFS IN THE MAKING

AGES 3–5: Help count the dough balls as you shape them.

Drizzle the glaze over cooled buns with a spoon.

AGES 5–10: Practice tearing off the dough into even pieces to make sure they bake evenly. If you have odd-size buns, some might burn while others are underbaked!

AGES 10+: This is an easy yeast-based baking project to try yourself.

Use a timer to make sure the yeast foams enough before continuing to mix the dough. Set the timer again when the dough needs to rise on the tray before baking. It's the difference between soft and fluffy, and hard pieces of bread!

FACT NOT FICTION

Currants began embedding themselves in English recipes in the 1500s when they began being imported from Greece. Sugar was still a luxury, so currants became a key sweetener. Today, these little dried fruits are still found in traditional British baked goods like fruitcakes, teacakes, and puddings.

MAKES ABOUT 12 CAKES

Winnie-the-Pooh's Sticky Honey Cakes

As soon as he got home, he went to the larder; and he stood on a chair, and took down a very large jar of honey from the top shelf. It had HUNNY *written on it, but, just to make sure, he took off the paper cover and looked at it, and it looked just like honey.*

—A. A. MILNE, *WINNIE-THE-POOH*

Pooh's adventures often find him with his head in a jar of honey, as this beloved bear is enchanted by the glistening, golden delight inside. Inspired by Pooh's love for this sweet, sticky treat, these mini cakes are soaked in a rich honey syrup. To allow enough time for the syrup to infuse through, these honey cakes are best prepared the night before, allowing ample time for the syrup to thoroughly soak into each cake, for a perfectly paw-licking experience the next day at teatime.

CAKES

1 cup unsalted butter, room temperature, plus more for greasing
½ cup granulated sugar
2 large eggs, room temperature
⅓ cup fresh orange juice
¾ teaspoon almond extract
1 cup semolina
½ cup all-purpose flour, plus more for dusting
2 teaspoons baking powder
¾ teaspoon sea salt
½ teaspoon ground allspice
⅛ teaspoon ground nutmeg
1 teaspoon ground cinnamon
½ cup almond meal

HONEY SYRUP

1 cup fresh orange juice
½ cup honey
5 whole cloves
¾ teaspoon ground cinnamon

TO MAKE THE CAKES: Preheat the oven to 350°F.

In a large bowl and using a handheld mixer, cream together the butter and granulated sugar on medium speed for 3 minutes until light and fluffy, scraping down the bowl halfway. Beat in the eggs one at a time. Add the orange juice and almond extract, mixing until well combined.

In another large bowl, sift together the semolina, all-purpose flour, baking powder, sea salt, allspice, nutmeg, and cinnamon, then stir in the almond meal.

Gradually stir the dry mixture into the wet mixture until fully incorporated.

Butter and then flour the inside of a 12-cup muffin tin. Then evenly scoop batter into each cup, smoothing the top with the back of a spoon.

Bake for 20 minutes, until a toothpick inserted into the center of a cake comes out clean. Let the cakes cool in the pan for 20 minutes. Carefully flip the cakes onto a baking sheet so the bottoms face up.

TO MAKE THE HONEY SYRUP: In a small saucepan over low heat, combine the orange juice, honey, cloves, and cinnamon. Bring the mixture to a simmer and let it cook for 5 minutes.

Turn off the heat and allow the syrup to cool for 1 hour to infuse the flavors. Strain the syrup through a fine-mesh strainer into a bowl to catch the cloves and sediment and then pour it evenly over the cakes.

Let the cakes soak for a minimum of 8 hours or overnight before serving. Store the honey cakes in an airtight container at room temperature for 3 to 4 days.

NOTE: Muffin tins are used in this recipe, as they are a staple in most kitchens. However, using alternative pans, such as friand or canelé pans, can add a touch of elegance when serving at afternoon tea.

HONEY

MAKES ABOUT 36 CONFECTIONS

Coconut Pineapple Petit Fours

They always had plenty to eat and drink; because Chee-Chee and Polynesia knew all the different kinds of fruits and vegetables that grow in the jungle, and where to find them . . . One day, while they were passing through a very thick part of the forest, Chee-Chee went ahead of them to look for cocoanuts.

—HUGH LOFTING, *THE STORY OF DOCTOR DOLITTLE*

Doctor Dolittle, a physician who prefers animals over human patients, learns to speak their languages with the help of his parrot and turns to veterinary practice. Gaining fame in the animal kingdom around the world, he is called to Africa to cure a monkey epidemic, setting sail with a crew of his favorite animals. Petit fours may be a world away from the land of the monkeys, but the eighteenth and nineteenth centuries saw a dramatic rise in botanical exploration, with adventurers exploring every nook and cranny of the globe and bringing home exotic trees, foods, and animals. Though introduced to the United Kingdom in earlier centuries, coconuts and pineapples were a rarity, making them both a curiosity and a luxury item. At the same time, afternoon teas were beginning to grow as a social event, and the popularity of small, elegant cakes and pastries served alongside tea became popular. Combining coconut jam and moist coconut flakes on top of a little bite-size cake for your own afternoon tea party is a nod to both the curiosity and popular pastimes of the Victorian era.

CAKES

1 cup unsalted butter, room temperature, plus more for greasing
1½ cups all-purpose flour, plus more for dusting
1 cup granulated sugar
1 teaspoon vanilla extract
3 large eggs, room temperature
¼ cup cornstarch
½ teaspoon cream of tartar
1 teaspoon baking powder
¼ teaspoon sea salt
¼ cup whole milk

PINEAPPLE JAM

One 15-ounce can pineapple slices in syrup, drained and syrup reserved
1½ cups granulated sugar

SERVING

¼ cup moist coconut flakes

TO MAKE THE CAKES: Preheat the oven to 350°F. Butter and flour the wells of a 24-cup mini muffin tin.

In the bowl of a stand mixer, or a large mixing bowl and using a handheld mixer, cream together the butter and sugar on medium speed for 2 minutes.

Turn off the mixer and scrape down the sides of the bowl. Add the vanilla and the eggs, one at a time, beating well after each addition until fully combined.

In a separate large bowl, sift together the all-purpose flour, cornstarch, cream of tartar, baking powder, and sea salt.

With the mixer on low speed, gradually add the dry ingredients to the wet ingredients. Mix until just combined. Pour in the whole milk and mix until fully incorporated.

Spoon heaping spoons of the batter into the prepared pan. Use the back of a spoon to smooth the tops evenly. Bake for 15 minutes, until golden brown.

Let the cakes cool in the pan for 10 minutes before transferring them to a wire rack to continue cooling. Repeat steps to bake any remaining batter.

Use a serrated bread knife to trim the tops flat, then carefully flip the cakes over so the bases become the tops of the mini cakes.

Continued on page 48

CHEFS IN THE MAKING

AGES 3–5: With clean hands, help butter muffin tins, but have an adult help make sure all the corners of are coated.

Have an adult hold a fine-mesh strainer with flour over the butter-coated muffin tins, and let you tap the strainer to dust. It might get a little messy!

TO MAKE THE PINEAPPLE JAM: In a small saucepan over medium heat, combine the pineapple syrup and sugar. Chop the pineapple pieces into ½-inch chunks and add them to the saucepan. Bring to a boil, then reduce the heat to medium low. Cook for 20 minutes, stirring frequently until the mixture has thickened and the pineapple pieces are translucent. To check the consistency, spoon a small amount onto a plate and let it sit for a minute. The jam should firm up and hold its shape instead of running when scooped.

Remove from the heat and let cool for 10 minutes. Transfer into a heatproof container and place in the refrigerator for 20 minutes to speed up cooling and help the jam set.

Spoon a teaspoon of jam onto each mini cake and lightly press the coconut flakes on top.

To store, place the cakes in an airtight container at room temperature for up to 3 days. Extra pineapple jam can be stored in an airtight container in the refrigerator for up to 2 weeks.

NOTE: Mini muffin tins have a 1½-inch base—slightly smaller than a traditional petit four pan—allowing enough space to hold a dollop of pineapple jam without it sliding off. Smaller than a muffin, the size makes for a dainty bite-size treat—a key consideration when selecting foods for a fancy tea party.

Crab-Apple Preserve

MAKES TWO 6-OUNCE JARS

Anne took off her hat meekly. Matthew came back presently and they sat down to supper. But Anne could not eat. In vain she nibbled at the bread and butter and pecked at the crab-apple preserve out of the little scalloped glass dish by her plate. She did not really make any headway at all.

—LUCY MAUD MONTGOMERY, *ANNE OF GREEN GABLES*

Anne Shirley has arrived at Green Gables in Avonlea, not only to find she's not the orphan boy that siblings Marilla and Matthew Cuthbert were expecting to help run their farm but at a place quite unprepared for her spirited presence. Marilla gets a taste of Anne's dramatic flare at the dinner table as Anne pecks at the dishes, among these a Crab-Apple Preserve. Recipes for Crab-Apple Preserves are common in old Canadian cookbooks, particularly on the East Coast where apples are typically ripe from mid-September to early October. To find crab apples nowadays either means to know someone with a tree on their property or to head out and enjoy searching for a local orchard that makes theirs available during the fall. This recipe creates a jelly preserve that can be made using various apple varieties and sizes, including green apples in case crab apples are unavailable.

INGREDIENTS

8 cups crab apples or 8 green apples
5 cups water
¼ cup apple cider vinegar
One 4-inch cinnamon stick
2 teaspoons whole cloves
2½ cups granulated sugar

Wash the crab apples, removing the blossom ends and stems. If using green apples, quarter and chop the apples into ¾-inch cubes, keeping the skin, seeds, and core intact.

Place in a large saucepan over medium heat and add water to cover.

Bring to a boil and then simmer, uncovered, for 20 minutes, until the apples are mushy.

Use a potato masher or the back of a fork to roughly mash the apples to help release the juice.

Transfer the mash to a cheesecloth bag hung over a clean saucepan. A fine-mesh strainer can be used instead.

Let strain for 1 hour, until you have 2 cups of strained liquid.

Use a spatula to gently scrape the outside bottom or sides of the cheesecloth bag or press the solids against the strainer to help release the liquid.

Discard the apple solids.

To the strained liquid, add the vinegar, cinnamon stick, whole cloves, and granulated sugar.

Bring the mixture to a boil and cook over medium heat for 10 minutes, stirring frequently. Skim off any scum that rises to the surface with a large spoon to keep the jelly clear.

Strain the mixture through a fine-mesh strainer set over a heatproof bowl to remove the spices.

Continued on page 50

Ladle the preserve into clean 6-ounce jars. Let cool, then close the jars and store in the refrigerator for up to 2 weeks.

NOTE: Use green apples instead of sweet, red apples when making preserve. Green apples contain more pectin, which helps the preserve set as a jelly properly. Green apples can be left to just use gravity to strain, but crab apples are even higher in pectin, so they need extra help to release the juice.

CHEFS IN THE MAKING

AGES 5–10: Time to get hands-on! Chop apples (with a safe knife and an adult's help) and measure out the sugar and vinegar.

AGES 10+: Dive into the basic skills of preserving fruit. With adult guidance, you'll learn the key steps of boiling and simmering, preserving the flavors of the season to enjoy long after it's gone, just like they did in the old days!

54
Cress Sandwiches and Potted Meat
The Wind in the Willows

57
Seed Cake
The Secret Garden

60
Mr. McGregor's Vegetable Patch Dip
The Tale of Peter Rabbit

62
Oat Cakes
Black Beauty

64
Rabbit's Savory Carrot Muffins
Winnie-the-Pooh

67
Paradise Picnic Pie
What Katy Did

70
Tappa Rolls
Peter and Wendy

Picnics and Light Luncheons

Katy, who sat in the middle, untied and lifted the lid of the largest basket, while all the rest peeped eagerly to see what was inside.

First came a great many ginger cakes. These were carefully laid on the grass to keep till wanted: buttered biscuit came next—three apiece, with slices of cold lamb laid in between; and last of all were a dozen hard-boiled eggs, and a layer of thick bread and butter sandwiched with corn-beef. Aunt Izzie had put up lunches for Paradise before, you see, and knew pretty well what to expect in the way of appetite.

Oh, how good everything tasted in that bower, with the fresh wind rustling the poplar leaves, sunshine and sweet wood-smells about them, and birds singing overhead!

—SUSAN COOLIDGE, *WHAT KATY DID*

Many of our favorite characters know that the simplest of meals can become the grandest when enjoyed in the open air. There's something about eating outdoors that makes every bite taste extraordinary, and unpacking a picnic basket is an exciting experience of its own, each wrapped dish waiting to be discovered.

After a morning spent pulling weeds from an overgrown garden and spotting the first peek of green pushing through the freshly warmed earth with Mary Lennox in *The Secret Garden*, a well-earned tea break feels all the more rewarding, especially when tea includes a traditional Seed Cake (page 57). Cress Sandwiches and Potted Meat (page 54) taste so satisfying after an afternoon spent drifting down the river with Mole and Rat in *The Wind in the Willows*. A quick snack from Mr. McGregor's garden in *The Tale of Peter Rabbit* reminds us just how delicious fresh vegetables can be—a moment we can capture in a crisp, flavorful vegetable dip (see page 60), perfect for keeping on hand for any outing.

The recipes in this chapter are inspired by the whimsical landscapes we've read about—from Neverland to the Hundred Acre Wood—and the gardens, vegetable patches, and burrows we wish we could visit. They're made to be enjoyed outdoors and many can be prepared ahead of time, ready for any spur-of-the-moment adventure.

From *Black Beauty* Oat Cakes (page 62) to Rabbit's Savory Carrot Muffins (page 64), these bites are made for slipping into pockets and baskets, so wherever you roam, whether it's a hidden garden, a quiet riverbank, or a sun-dappled field, there's always something delicious waiting to be enjoyed.

Cress Sandwiches and Potted Meat

"Hold hard a minute, then!" said the Rat. He looped the painter through a ring in his landing-stage, climbed up into his hole above, and after a short interval reappeared staggering under a fat, wicker luncheon-basket.

"Shove that under your feet," he observed to the Mole, as he passed it down into the boat. Then he untied the painter and took the sculls again.

"What's inside it?" asked the Mole, wriggling with curiosity.

"There's cold chicken inside it," replied the Rat briefly; "coldtonguecoldhamcoldbeefpickledgherkinssaladfrenchrollscresssandwichespottedmeatgingerbeerlemonadesodawater——"

—KENNETH GRAHAME, *THE WIND IN THE WILLOWS*

After busily preparing his home for spring, Mole meets Rat, and together they drift down the river, enjoying the fresh spring air. His new friend, ever the prepared host, presents a fat, wicker luncheon basket, packed to the brim with an array of picnic essentials. As Mole shares his jubilation, we partake in his joy, which may stir in us a longing to pack a picnic of our own to celebrate spring's return. Freshly plucked from the shallow riverbanks, watercress has a mild peppery flavor that is best enjoyed with nothing more than bread, butter, salt, and pepper to allow the delicate flavor to be tasted. Potted meat—rich, moist, and savory—is far removed from today's supermarket varieties but perfectly complements French rolls and is a great addition to your picnic basket.

WATERCRESS SANDWICHES

2 cups loosely packed watercress, torn into 3-inch pieces (including some stems)
⅔ teaspoon sea salt
¼ cup unsalted butter, room temperature
8 slices whole wheat bread

POTTED MEAT

6 tablespoons olive oil
1½ pounds chuck pot roast
1½ cups beef stock
2 tablespoons lightly packed light brown sugar
3 tablespoons apple cider vinegar
½ teaspoon mustard powder
1 teaspoon onion powder
1 teaspoon garlic powder
2 teaspoons ground black pepper
½ teaspoon sea salt

TO MAKE THE WATERCRESS SANDWICHES: Thoroughly wash the watercress and pat dry. Place the watercress in a bowl, sprinkle with sea salt, and toss to combine.

Evenly spread butter on each slice of bread. Divide the salted watercress evenly across four slices of buttered bread. Close the sandwiches with the remaining slices of bread, ensuring the buttered side is facing the watercress.

TO MAKE THE POTTED MEAT: Preheat the oven to 325°F.

Pour half of the olive oil into the bottom of a Dutch oven, then place the beef on top. Drizzle the remaining olive oil over the beef. Bake the beef for 30 minutes to brown, uncovered.

Add the stock, brown sugar, vinegar, mustard powder, onion powder, garlic powder, pepper, and sea salt to the pot. Stir to combine. Return the pot to the oven and cook for 2 hours, covered, until the chuck pot roast is fork-tender. A fork inserted into the meat should twist easily, and the roast should begin to fall apart.

Remove the pot from the oven and let the beef cool for 15 minutes. Transfer the beef to a food processor along with ¼ cup of the stock from the pot. Process until smooth and slightly loose in texture.

Continued on page 56

CHEFS IN THE MAKING

AGES 5–10+: Everyone can learn the art of sandwich making! Tear the watercress, spread butter, and carefully assemble your sandwich with simple, tasty fillings.

FACT NOT FICTION

Just as the warm spring sun is a welcome sight to Mole after being underground, the first shoots of watercress, which grew wild in the shallow riverbanks of the English countryside, would have been a welcome sight after a long winter for many centuries, a sign of spring arriving.

Transfer the mixture to four glass jars and pour the remaining liquid from the pot evenly into each jar to fill the remaining air gaps. Place in the refrigerator to cool and set. The cooled fat layer will create a natural seal protecting the meat from oxygen. Use within 4 days or freeze any excess portions for 3 months.

NOTE: Potted meat is a great way to use up leftover chuck pot roast. This full recipe yields four 7-ounce jars of potted beef, but this recipe for slow-cooked chuck pot roast is also an affordable and delicious dinner option. For a meal for two, serve three-quarters of the chuck roast, paired with potatoes and greens. Then purée the remaining meat in a food processor with 1 tablespoon of stock to fill one jar. Store it in the refrigerator for a quick, flavorful spread to enjoy with mustard, fresh bread, and a side salad throughout the week.

MAKE ONE 7-INCH ROUND CAKE

Seed Cake

They saw the robin carry food to his mate two or three times, and it was so suggestive of afternoon tea that Colin felt they must have some. . . .

It was an agreeable idea, easily carried out, and when the white cloth was spread upon the grass, with hot tea and buttered toast and crumpets, a delightfully hungry meal was eaten, and several birds on domestic errands paused to inquire what was going on and were led into investigating crumbs with great activity.

—FRANCES HODGSON BURNETT, *THE SECRET GARDEN*

In the confines of a secret garden on a country estate, nestled in the Yorkshire moors in England, an afternoon outing stirs the appetite of Mary, Colin, and Dickon. Given that their spread captures a typical British afternoon tea, the cake mentioned is likely a traditional Seed Cake. Caraway, known for its nutty, citrusy flavor with notes of anise, like a light-flavored fennel, was a favorite at British tables, where it was commonly used in caraway comfits—sugar-coated caraway seeds—served at the end of meals to aid digestion. The simplicity of making seed cake—creaming, sifting, pouring, and baking—makes it an ideal treat to prepare ahead, ready to enjoy leisurely afternoons in hidden gardens.

INGREDIENTS

¾ cup granulated sugar
1 cup butter, room temperature, plus more for the pan
2 large eggs, room temperature
3 large egg yolks, room temperature
½ teaspoon vanilla extract
1¾ cups all-purpose flour
1 tablespoon plus ½ teaspoon baking powder
¾ teaspoon sea salt
A splash of brandy (optional)
3 tablespoons caraway seeds
1 tablespoon grated lemon zest
¼ cup candied peel (see page 106)

Preheat the oven to 375°F.

In the bowl of a stand mixer, or a large mixing bowl if using a hand mixer, beat the granulated sugar and butter on medium speed for 2 minutes until light in color, scraping down the bowl halfway through.

Mix in the eggs, egg yolks, and vanilla until combined.

In a large bowl, sift together the all-purpose flour, baking powder, and sea salt.

Start mixing at low speed and add the flour mixture until combined, then increase to medium speed and beat for 6 minutes until the mixture is fluffy and white.

If desired, add a splash of brandy for an authentic taste.

Mix in the caraway seeds, lemon zest, and candied peel until evenly distributed throughout the batter.

Butter a 7-inch round cake pan and line it with parchment paper. Scoop the cake batter into the prepared pan, spreading it evenly.

Bake for 55 minutes, until the top is a deep golden brown and a skewer inserted into the center comes out clean.

Continued on page 59

CHEFS IN THE MAKING

AGES 3–5: Everyone can get involved with this activity. Grease the cake pan with butter using your fingers for a fun, hands-on experience.

AGES 5–10: Zest the lemon with a little help, crack the eggs, and line the cake pan with parchment paper. Use the hand mixer on low speed with adult guidance for a smooth, fluffy batter.

AGES 10+: Once the cake is baked, use a toothpick to check if it's ready to come out of the oven.

Remove the cake from the oven and allow it to cool in the pan for a few minutes before transferring it to a wire rack to cool completely. Seed cake can be stored in an airtight container at room temperature for up to 5 days.

PAIRS WELL WITH: To re-create Mary, Colin, and Dickon's spread, pair this recipe with Garden Crumpets (page 35) for your own secret garden experience.

MAKES
I CUP DIP

Mr. McGregor's Vegetable Patch Dip

First he ate some lettuces and some French beans; and then he ate some radishes;
And then, feeling rather sick, he went to look for some parsley.
But round the end of a cucumber frame, whom should he meet but Mr. McGregor!

—BEATRIX POTTER, *THE TALE OF PETER RABBIT*

Young Peter Rabbit mischievously romps through Mr. McGregor's garden, nibbling his way through a variety of fresh vegetables and herbs. And who can blame him? Fresh produce picked straight from the garden tastes completely different from store-bought food, and a visit to a farmers' market is the next best thing to eating your way through Mr. McGregor's garden. Load up on fresh herbs, radishes, and cucumbers to create a versatile dip that can be used as a sandwich spread or a delicious dip next to platters of raw carrots, celery, and plain crackers.

INGREDIENTS

One 7- to 8-inch Persian cucumber, seeded
¾ teaspoon sea salt, divided
½ cup Greek yogurt
8 medium-large radishes, tails and stems removed
2 medium garlic cloves, minced
1 cup lightly packed fresh parsley
1 tablespoon chopped fresh chives
¼ cup fresh lemon juice
Zest of 1 medium lemon
¼ teaspoon ground white pepper
One 8-ounce package cream cheese, room temperature

Sprinkle ½ teaspoon of sea salt across both seeded cucumber halves. Let sit for 10 minutes.

Pour the Greek yogurt into a fine-mesh strainer placed over a measuring cup and let sit for 10 minutes to drain the excess liquid.

Rinse the cucumber halves and roughly chop and squeeze them, discarding the liquid.

Place the chopped cucumber, radishes, and remaining ¼ teaspoon of sea salt in a food processor and pulse for 10 seconds until finely chopped. Let sit for 5 minutes then squeeze to remove excess liquid and discard the juice.

Add the minced garlic, parsley, chives, lemon juice, lemon zest, white pepper, cream cheese, and the strained Greek yogurt to the food processor. Pulse to combine all the ingredients.

Let the mixture sit for a minimum of 8 hours or overnight in the refrigerator to allow the flavors to infuse.

The dip can be stored in the refrigerator for 3 days in an airtight container.

PARSLEY

MAKES 12 OAT CAKES

Oat Cakes

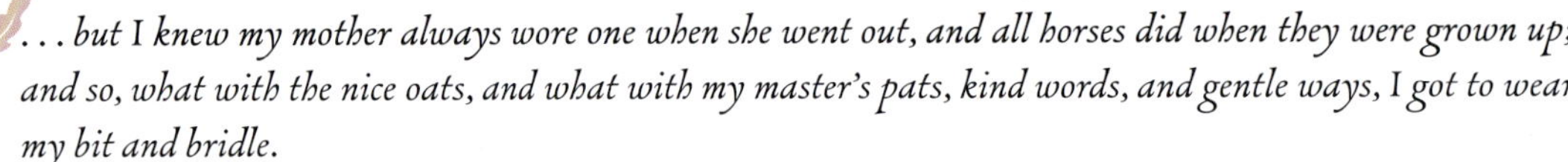

. . . but I knew my mother always wore one when she went out, and all horses did when they were grown up; and so, what with the nice oats, and what with my master's pats, kind words, and gentle ways, I got to wear my bit and bridle.

—ANNA SEWELL, *BLACK BEAUTY*

Through the eyes of young horse Black Beauty, we see the varied nature of humankind—from the kind and gentle to the cruel or careless. Black Beauty's early experiences were only the former, where kindness was as nourishing as the oats he was fed. Oats, a wholesome and rustic grain, have been a cornerstone of sustenance for centuries, not just for horses in nineteenth-century England but also for communities across Scotland, Northern England, and Ireland.

INGREDIENTS

1½ cups gluten-free old-fashioned rolled oats (not instant)
¼ teaspoon sea salt
2 tablespoons raw sugar
¼ cup hot (not boiling) water
1 teaspoon active dry yeast
1 tablespoon vegetable oil

CHEFS IN THE MAKING

AGES 5–10: Help by rolling out the dough, cutting out the oat cakes with round cutters, and placing them on the baking sheet.

AGES 10+: This is an easy recipe to make yourself. Ask an adult for help when using the oven.

Preheat the oven to 350°F.

Place the rolled oats in a food processor and process for 30 seconds until a fine-coarse oat flour is achieved.

Sprinkle 1 teaspoon of oat flour on the counter to dust. Stir the sea salt into the remaining oat flour.

In a measuring cup, stir together the raw sugar, hot water, and dry yeast. Let sit for 10 minutes.

Stir the vegetable oil into the yeast mixture before adding the wet mixture to the oat flour. Mix until combined into a dough.

Roll out the dough on the flour-dusted counter to less than ¼ inch thick. The dough should be dry enough to not stick to the counter.

Cut the dough into 2½-inch circles, place on an unlined baking sheet, and position on the middle rack in the oven. Bake for 15 minutes until golden brown, then flip the oat cakes and bake for an additional 5 minutes until they turn a light shade of brown and look crispy.

Turn off the oven, open the oven door slightly, and let the oat cakes cool for 1 hour.

Oat cakes are easily prepared in advance. Store in an airtight container for up to 2 weeks at room temperature, ready to serve with cheese and cold meats for impromptu meals.

PAIRS WELL WITH: Perfect whether accompanying a hearty Slow-Cooked Soup (page 84) or served with a cheese platter, pair with hard cheeses, apple slices, and a dollop of savory jam such as caramelized onion jam (see page 38) for a light, outdoor lunch with a rustic touch.

MAKES
12 MUFFINS

Rabbit's Savory Carrot Muffins

Pooh always liked a little something at eleven o'clock in the morning, and he was very glad to see Rabbit getting out the plates and mugs; and when Rabbit said, "Honey or condensed milk with your bread?" he was so excited that he said, "Both," and then, so as not to seem greedy, he added, "But don't bother about the bread, please." And for a long time after that he said nothing . . . until at last, humming to himself in a rather sticky voice, he got up, shook Rabbit lovingly by the paw, and said that he must be going on.

—A.A. MILNE, *WINNIE-THE-POOH*

When Pooh peeks into Rabbit's cozy burrow, he's certain of three things: Rabbit means company, food, and an audience for the hums he has made up during his morning Stoutness Exercises—*Rum-tum-tum-tiddle-um*. Ever the gracious host, Rabbit offers what he has, all staples of Pooh's favorite treats. However, to avoid your guests getting stuck on their way out, as Pooh does when he departs, opt for something healthier like savory muffins. Thoughtfully and meticulously, like Rabbit himself, use a burst of initial heat in the oven to give the muffins a beautifully rounded top, then reduce the temperature to cook through evenly without burning. These muffins make an ideal lunchtime offering for any visitor.

INGREDIENTS

1 cup all-purpose flour, plus more for dusting
1 cup whole wheat flour
3½ teaspoons baking powder
¼ cup granulated sugar
½ teaspoon sea salt
1 cup grated Parmesan cheese
1 tablespoon finely chopped fresh sage
½ cup chopped fresh parsley leaves
1 large egg, room temperature
¼ cup olive oil
1 cup whole milk
1 tablespoon lemon zest
2 tablespoons fresh lemon juice
2 cups grated carrots
Butter, for greasing

Preheat the oven to 425°F.

In the bowl of a stand mixer, or a large mixing bowl if using a hand mixer, sift together the all-purpose flour, whole wheat flour, and baking powder.

Stir in the granulated sugar and sea salt.

Toss the grated Parmesan, sage, and parsley into the dry mixture to coat evenly.

In another large bowl, whisk together the egg, olive oil, whole milk, lemon zest, and lemon juice.

Add the grated carrots to the wet mixture and stir until combined.

Pour the wet ingredients into the dry ingredients and stir until just incorporated. Avoid overmixing.

Continued on page 66

CHEFS IN THE MAKING

AGES 5–10: Both the cheese and carrots need to be grated in this recipe. You can help by using a box grater with supervision.

The butter helps the flour stick to the tin, but the flour keeps the muffins from sticking so they slide out easily after baking. Help by making sure the pan is evenly buttered then dusted.

AGES 10+: Watch the oven to see how the high temperature at the beginning of baking helps the centers of the muffins rise quickly. Help keep the muffins from burning by making sure the temperature is turned down after 10 minutes.

Butter and flour a 12-cup muffin tin to prevent the muffins from sticking before evenly spooning in the batter.

Bake at 425°F for 10 minutes, then reduce the heat to 400°F and bake for an additional 12 minutes, until a toothpick inserted into the center of the muffin comes out clean.

Allow to cool for 10 minutes before serving. To store, let cool completely before placing in an airtight container at room temperature for up to 3 days.

MAKES
12 MINI PIES

Paradise Picnic Pie

Each mouthful was a pleasure; and when the last crumb had vanished, Katy produced the second basket, and there, oh, delightful surprise! were seven little pies—molasses pies, baked in saucers—each with a brown top and crisp candified edge, which tasted like toffy and lemon-peel, and all sorts of good things mixed up together.

There was a general shout. Even demure Cecy was pleased, and Dorry and John kicked their heels on the ground in a tumult of joy. Seven pairs of hands were held out at once toward the basket; seven sets of teeth went to work without a moment's delay. In an incredibly short time every vestige of the pie had disappeared, and a blissful stickiness pervaded the party.

—SUSAN COOLIDGE, *WHAT KATY DID*

The secret haven dubbed "Paradise" by the Carr children offers adventure for Katy, her siblings, and their friend Cecy, with many paths and secret nooks to explore, sparking both their imaginations and appetites. Aunt Izzie, well-versed in the art of picnic preparation, packs a basket with a feast to fuel their adventures—ginger cakes, buttered biscuits with cold lamb, hard-boiled eggs, and thick corned beef sandwiches—but the true treasure is hidden in a second basket: molasses pies. To re-create a pie that tastes of toffee and lemon peel like Aunt Izzie's original recipe, don't forget to reach for light unsulphured molasses.

PIE DOUGH

1¼ cups all-purpose flour
½ teaspoon sea salt
7 tablespoons cold unsalted butter, chopped into ¾-inch cubes
3 tablespoons cold water

PARADISE PIES

¾ cup packed dark brown sugar
¼ cup light unsulphured molasses or golden syrup

Tip: Using a darker molasses will result in a bitter, overwhelming flavor—far from the sweetness of Katy's childhood treat. If light, unsulphured molasses isn't available, substitute 2 tablespoons of golden syrup and 2 tablespoons of dark treacle.

¼ cup melted unsalted butter
1 large egg
2 tablespoons fresh lemon juice
1 teaspoon lemon zest
1 teaspoon vanilla extract
Pinch sea salt

TO MAKE THE PIE DOUGH: In a food processor, combine the flour and sea salt and pulse to combine.

Turn on the processor and add the cold unsalted butter cubes. Pulse for 10 seconds until the flour and butter combine into a wet crumb.

With the processor running, pour the cold water in a steady stream through the tube feeder until the dough forms into a ball.

Wrap the dough in parchment paper and place it in the refrigerator for 1 hour.

TO MAKE THE PARADISE PIES: Preheat the oven to 350°F.

Dust a clean kitchen counter with flour and roll out the pie dough until it is ¼-inch thick, then cut out twelve 4-inch circles and line the muffin tins.

In a medium bowl, stir together the brown sugar, light molasses, melted butter, egg, lemon juice, lemon zest, vanilla, and sea salt.

Pour the mixture evenly into the prepared dough-lined tin, filling them only halfway. Overfilling these pies is a recipe for a sticky dilemma, as molasses, once candied and hardened, becomes a challenge to clean.

Pies can be stored in an airtight container at room temperature for 3 days or in the refrigerator for up to 1 week.

Continued on page 68

Bake for 25 minutes, until the tops are browned and the edges have a candied appearance. Allow the pies to cool slightly before serving.

NOTE: In Paradise, these molasses pies are baked in saucers, the small, shallow plates teacups rest on. To re-create an authentic experience, make sure the saucers are oven-safe, which will be printed on the bottom of the saucer. Use ¼ cup of filling for each pie, which will make five saucer-size pies. Use the saucer itself to trace a circle on the dough with a knife to cut the dough to size.

CHEFS IN THE MAKING

AGES 3–5: Help press the dough into muffin tins or saucers.

AGES 5–10+: Use cookie cutters or a saucer to trace and cut out dough circles.

It's a sticky job, but practice carefully spooning the filling into prepared dough shells. An adult can help make sure they aren't overfilled.

MAKES
10 ROLLS

Tappa Rolls

Their chief food was roasted bread-fruit, yams, coconuts, baked pig, mammee-apples, tappa rolls and bananas, washed down with calabashes of poe-poe; but you never exactly knew whether there would be a real meal or just a make-believe, it all depended upon Peter's whim.

—J. M. BARRIE, *PETER AND WENDY*

Far from the cobblestone streets of London, the adventures of Neverland are as unpredictable and spirited as Peter Pan himself. Neverland's feasts draw generously from tropical bounty—from breadfruit to yams. Though many of the ingredients mentioned are familiar, "tappa" requires a flight of imagination. After a morning filled with adventure alongside Peter Pan and his crew, transform tropical ingredients into a crepe with sweet-savory fillings for lunch. The crepes, made from a batter of overripe bananas and coconut milk, roll around pieces of bacon—the "baked pig" of the Neverland feast—and are smothered in a sweet and savory sauce that captures South Pacific flavors.

BANANA KETCHUP

2 garlic cloves
1 overripe banana
1 cup white wine vinegar
½ cup lightly packed light brown sugar
1 tablespoon soy sauce
1 teaspoon ground ginger
½ teaspoon ground cinnamon
1 small yellow onion, peeled
⅛ teaspoon red pepper flakes

BANANA CREPES

1 large egg
1 cup coconut milk
¾ cup mashed overripe banana
2 tablespoons granulated sugar
1 cup all-purpose flour
¼ teaspoon sea salt
5 tablespoons unsalted butter

SERVING

10 strips cooked bacon (see page 24)
1 large mango, peeled, seeded, and sliced

TO MAKE THE BANANA KETCHUP: In a food processor, blend together all the ingredients until smooth. Transfer the mixture to a small saucepan and place over medium-low heat.

Cook for 5 minutes, then reduce the heat to low and cook for an additional 25 minutes, stirring every 5 minutes until the sauce thickens. Remove from the heat and let cool before using.

TO MAKE THE BANANA CREPES: In a food processor or blender, combine the egg, coconut milk, banana, granulated sugar, flour, and sea salt. Blend for 15 seconds until smooth.

Heat a 9-inch frying pan over medium-low heat for 1 minute. Then melt 1 tablespoon of butter in it for 30 seconds. Pour in ¼ cup of batter and tilt the pan to spread it evenly into a circle.

Adjust the heat to low and cook for 3 minutes, until the edges of the crepe have set and begin to lift slightly from the pan. You should be able to slide a spatula underneath without any batter sticking. Gently lift the edge to check that the bottom is lightly golden, then flip the crepe to cook the other side for another 2 minutes until the underside is golden. Remove the crepe from the pan and set aside on a plate.

Repeat with the remaining batter, adding another tablespoon of butter after every two crepes. If needed, briefly remove the pan from the heat halfway through to cool slightly.

TO SERVE: Evenly spread each crepe with 1 tablespoon of banana ketchup, then add a strip of bacon and a thin slice of mango, before rolling each crepe to close and serve.

74
Bubble and Squeak
The Wind in the Willows

77
Nutkin's Nut Loaf
The Tale of Squirrel Nutkin

80
Corn Dodgers
The Adventures of Huckleberry Finn

83
Greens

84
Slow-Cooked Soup
The Swiss Family Robinson

86
Croûte au Fromage
Heidi

88
Poultry Pie
Treasure Island

91
A Welcome Supper
The Railway Children

Hearty Meals

There never was such a Christmas dinner as they had that day. The fat turkey was a sight to behold, when Hannah sent him up, stuffed, browned, and decorated. So was the plum pudding, which melted in one's mouth, likewise the jellies, in which Amy reveled like a fly in a honeypot.

—LOUISA MAY ALCOTT, *LITTLE WOMEN*

Nothing tastes more satisfying than a warm meal after a long journey or a trying experience. Jim Hawkins in *Treasure Island* knows this well, after a perilous night evading pirates when he finds solace in a rich Poultry Pie (page 88).

No matter how our characters travel—by sea, land, or rail—a shared meal with family offers a chance to gather and reconnect, whether that's around A Welcome Supper (page 91) from *The Railway Children* or a Slow-Cooked Soup (page 84) from *The Swiss Family Robinson*.

Sometimes the simplest meals provide the deepest comfort. In *The Wind in the Willows*, Toad discovers that a steaming plate of Bubble and Squeak (page 74) has the power to lift his spirits. Even the most basic ingredients, when cooked with care, can soothe.

And the recipes for hearty meals in this chapter aren't just about soothing; they're also a way to celebrate—from the experiences in your life to the changing of the seasons. Nutkin's Nut Loaf (page 77), inspired by the squirrels' autumn harvesting in *The Tale of Squirrel Nutkin*, captures the essence of the crisp air and golden leaves with its mix of nuts, herbs, and root vegetables.

Bubble and Squeak

It was bubble-and-squeak, between two plates, and its fragrance filled the narrow cell. The penetrating smell of cabbage reached the nose of Toad as he lay prostrate in his misery on the floor, and gave him the idea for a moment that perhaps life was not such a blank and desperate thing as he had imagined.

—KENNETH GRAHAME, *THE WIND IN THE WILLOWS*

Toad's penchant for reckless driving finally gets him in hot water. After a misadventure involving a stolen automobile lands him in jail, he wallows in self-pity until the jailer's daughter comes in bearing a simple yet nourishing dish of Bubble and Squeak. How comforting the scent of this steaming plate of food must have been to have such a transformative power over Toad's mood! Named for the delightful sounds emanating from the pot as it cooks, bubble and squeak traditionally uses leftovers from a hearty dinner—beef, cabbage, potatoes, and onion. The corned beef and potatoes can be prepared the night before and stored in the refrigerator overnight, whereas the cabbage keeps this dish fresh and crisp.

CORNED BEEF AND POTATOES

8 cups cold water
1 cup apple cider vinegar
2 pounds corned beef brisket, rinsed
2 bay leaves
4 whole cloves
1 teaspoon whole black peppercorns
1 large yellow onion, halved
1½ pounds yellow baby potatoes

BUBBLE AND SQUEAK

8 cups water
1 teaspoon kosher salt
½ head green cabbage
¼ cup unsalted butter, divided
1 large yellow onion, diced
¼ cup apple cider vinegar
1 teaspoon sea salt
1 teaspoon ground black pepper

TO MAKE THE CORNED BEEF AND POTATOES: In a large Dutch oven over high heat, combine the cold water and apple cider vinegar. Add the corned beef, bay leaves, cloves, peppercorns, and onion.

Use a sharp knife to remove any sprouts or rough spots from the potatoes and then add them to the pot. Cover and bring to a rolling boil, 15 minutes.

Reduce the heat to low and cook for 30 minutes until a fork slides easily into the potatoes with no resistance. They should be tender but still hold their shape without falling apart. Transfer the potatoes to a bowl, let cool for 15 minutes, then refrigerate until serving.

Continue cooking the meat in the pot, covered, for another 2 hours until the corned beef is fork-tender. Remove the meat and let it cool on a cutting board.

TO MAKE THE BUBBLE AND SQUEAK: Empty and rinse the Dutch oven, then return it to the stove over high heat. Add the water and kosher salt and bring to a boil.

Rinse and core the cabbage, then cut it into ¼-inch shreds. Add the cabbage to the boiling water and cook for 10 minutes with the lid off.

Turn off the heat and transfer the cabbage to a colander to drain, pressing the cabbage with a wooden spoon to release any excess liquid. Transfer it to a large mixing bowl and cover with a large plate to keep the cabbage warm.

Chop the corned beef and potatoes into ½-inch cubes.

Place the Dutch oven over medium heat and melt half the butter for 1 minute.

Dab the cold potatoes with a clean kitchen towel to remove any moisture before adding them to the pan in a single layer. Cook for 10 minutes, until the undersides are lightly golden in spots and starting to crisp, then flip them to finish browning for a further 5 minutes.

Continued on page 76

CHEFS IN THE MAKING

AGES 5–10+: After adults cook the corned beef the first time, the beef will become softer as it cooks. Ask the adults to cut off a thin slice at the 1-hour mark, 2-hour mark and 2½-hour mark for you to try so you can taste and see how the texture changes as the meat cooks.

Add the remaining butter and melt. Add the onion and cook for 5 minutes until translucent and beginning to brown, stirring halfway. Stir in the beef and cook for 10 minutes, then flip and stir halfway through. Add the apple cider vinegar and use a wooden spoon to deglaze the pan, scraping up any browned bits stuck to the bottom.

Roughly chop any large pieces of the cooked cabbage and squeeze out any remaining water before adding to the pan. Sprinkle with sea salt and pepper, stir, and cook for 3 minutes to warm through.

Divide evenly among bowls, let cool for 5 minutes, and serve. Leftovers can be stored in an airtight container in the refrigerator for up to 3 days.

MAKES 1 LOAF

Nutkin's Nut Loaf

The squirrels searched for nuts all over the island and filled their little sacks.

But Nutkin gathered oak-apples—yellow and scarlet—and sat upon a beech-stump playing marbles, and watching the door of old Mr. Brown.

—BEATRIX POTTER, *THE TALE OF SQUIRREL NUTKIN*

When autumn unfurls its tapestry of golden leaves, it marks the perfect season for hazelnut harvesting. Ready to gather for the winter, a family of squirrels seeks permission from the owl, old Mr. Brown, to gather nuts on his island. All except Nutkin, a cheeky red squirrel who instead taunts and riddles to stir the old owl. Just as Nutkin's family is diligent in gathering nuts, gather your own autumn harvest with a variety of hearty root vegetables and nuts, then pay the simple ingredients special attention to transform them, capturing the best of the season. Resist the urge to simply toss everything together: The onions are caramelized to unlock their sweetness, the parsnips are roasted while preserving texture, and the walnuts are fried to bring out their nuttiness and provide a satisfying crunch.

INGREDIENTS

2 medium parsnips, chopped into ½-inch cubes (2 cups)
1 tablespoon all-purpose flour
2 tablespoons honey
⅓ cup water
5 tablespoons unsalted butter, divided
2 medium onions, finely chopped (2¼ cups)
¼ cup raw sugar
3 tablespoons balsamic vinegar
¼ cup lightly packed fresh sage leaves
1½ cups walnut pieces
½ cup crushed hazelnut pieces
½ teaspoon sea salt
2 cups fresh breadcrumbs
1 cup freshly grated sharp cheddar cheese
1 tablespoon finely chopped fresh rosemary leaves

Preheat the oven to 400°F.

In a small bowl, toss the parsnip cubes with the flour and place them in a small roasting pan. Drizzle with the honey and pour the water into the bottom of the pan.

Roast for 20 minutes. Turn off the oven, leave the door ajar, and keep the parsnips warm.

Meanwhile, in a 9-inch frying pan, melt 2 tablespoons of butter over medium-low heat.

Add the onions, stir to coat, and cook for 5 minutes, stirring occasionally.

Stir in the raw sugar and cook for an additional 5 minutes, stirring occasionally.

Transfer the onions to the roasting pan with the parsnips and return the pan to the oven.

Add the balsamic vinegar to the frying pan over medium-low heat and scrape up any caramelized bits with a wooden spoon. Pour this balsamic glaze into the roasting pan.

Melt 1 tablespoon of butter in the frying pan and fry the whole sage leaves for 2 minutes until crispy. Transfer them to a cutting board to cool.

Continued on page 78

In the frying pan over medium-low heat, melt the remaining 2 tablespoons of butter. Add the walnut and hazelnut pieces, stir to coat, and lower the heat. Cook for 5 minutes, stirring occasionally, until browned.

Transfer the nuts to the cutting board to cool slightly, then roughly chop and lightly crush the sage leaves.

Stir the nuts and sage into the parsnip mixture and add the sea salt, breadcrumbs, cheddar cheese, and finely chopped rosemary until combined and the cheese has melted.

Line a standard loaf pan with parchment paper. Scoop in the parsnip mixture, pressing it down firmly. Allow to cool, then slice and serve. Store leftovers in the refrigerator in an airtight container for up to 3 days.

CHEFS IN THE MAKING

AGES 3–5: Help tear bread into pieces for breadcrumbs.

AGES 5–10: There are lots of ingredients in this list! Read out the ingredients to make sure everything is ready before starting. This is also a recipe in patience, so help by making sure the ingredients are prepared and organized by the different stages.

AGES 10+: Help by looking after the roasting stage at the beginning of the recipe, while an adult can look after the cooking steps on the stove. You can step back in to combine all the ingredients together at the end and scoop them into the loaf pan to finish.

MAKES
20 DODGERS

Corn Dodgers

I hadn't had a bite to eat since yesterday; so Jim he got out some corn-dodgers and buttermilk, and pork and cabbage, and greens there ain't nothing in the world so good, when it's cooked right and whilst I eat my supper we talked, and had a good time.

—MARK TWAIN, *THE ADVENTURES OF HUCKLEBERRY FINN*

Huckleberry Finn's journey along the Mississippi River is punctuated by moments of simplicity and comfort against the backdrop of deep-seated social issues and personal turmoil. Famished and weary after recent experiences, both Jim's comforting hug and Southern food are a moment of solace and recovery. Corn Dodgers, a staple of the South, are traditionally crafted from cornmeal and cooked over an open fire. Though modern stoves can't replicate the distinct flavor of cooking outdoors, good-quality smoked bacon fat captures that depth of flavor. And as the flavor of the Corn Dodgers depends entirely on the buttermilk and bacon fat that it soaks up, be sure to use the best-quality bacon you can find.

RENDERED BACON FAT

1½ cups roughly chopped smoked bacon fat

3 cups water, divided

CORN DODGERS

2¼ cups medium-grind cornmeal (whole grain, stone ground), divided

1 teaspoon sea salt

1⅓ cups buttermilk (see note)

¼ cup plus 1½ tablespoons rendered bacon fat or bacon drippings, divided

TO RENDER THE BACON FAT: In a 9-inch heavy-bottomed frying pan over medium heat, cook the chopped bacon fat and ½ cup of water to prevent the fat from frying and browning. Cook uncovered for 20 minutes. The water will boil off and the sound will shift from bubbling to frying.

Strain the fat through a fine-mesh strainer into a heatproof measuring cup, pressing the fat pieces with a wooden spoon to extract as much fat as possible. Return the remaining solid bits to the pan with the remaining 2½ cups of water and repeat the process to melt any remaining fat.

Let the fat cool for 15 minutes to separate from any remaining liquid and firm up. Scoop off the solidified fat and set aside to use. The crispy bits left behind can be used as a topping for the Greens (page 83).

TO MAKE THE CORN DODGERS: In a medium heavy-bottomed saucepan, combine 2 cups of cornmeal, the sea salt, buttermilk, and ¼ cup of rendered bacon fat over medium-low heat. Stir constantly for 5 minutes until the mixture thickens into a porridge-like consistency.

Remove from the heat and let cool for 15 minutes, stirring occasionally to release the heat.

With wet hands, scoop 2 tablespoons of the mixture into your palm and squeeze it into an oval shape, about 2 inches long and 1 inch thick. Repeat with the remaining mixture.

Heat ½ tablespoon of rendered bacon fat in a heavy-bottomed frying pan over medium-low heat for 1 minute to melt.

Continued on page 82

Roll each corn dodger in the remaining ¼ cup of cornmeal to coat, then place half in the pan. Fry for 4 minutes on one side, then use a wooden spatula to roll the dodgers and fry for 3 minutes and roll once more to fry any remaining uncooked surface area for another 3 minutes for a crispy shell with a soft interior.

Remove the pan from the heat for 2 minutes to lower the temperature to prevent burning the next batch. Add the remaining rendered bacon fat to the pan and repeat cooking the remaining dodgers.

PAIRS WELL WITH: Serve the corn dodgers alongside Greens (page 83) and slices of ham. Continue your *Adventures of Huckleberry Finn*–inspired meal with a Fried Egg Feast (page 24).

NOTE: Buttermilk is traditionally the liquid left behind after cream has been churned into butter, but if you don't have any in the refrigerator, you can make your own at home by adding an acid to milk. Combine ¾ cup of whole milk with 1 tablespoon of fresh lemon juice and let sit for 15 minutes before using.

CHEFS IN THE MAKING

AGES 3–5: Help by rolling shaped corn dodgers in cornmeal.

Help wash and tear greens into smaller pieces.

AGES 5–10: Help scoop and shape dodgers with wet hands.

AGES 10+: Stir the cornmeal mixture as it thickens on the stovetop (with supervision).

Help adults mix and shape the corn dodgers before they cook them on the stove.

FACT NOT FICTION

Corn pone, Corn Dodgers, and cornbread—what's the difference? Corn pone is similar to cornbread but shaped into individual patties and cooked in a skillet. The definitions for Corn Dodgers vary across the South. Where Huckleberry Finn's story is based, they were small oval cakes made from thick cornmeal batter that are fried, compared to the boiled dumplings common in other areas of the United States.

Greens

You can't truly enjoy Corn Dodgers without the perfect accompaniment—Greens! Jim and Huck likely foraged for wild greens along the Mississippi River; however, turnip greens or collard greens are typically used as staples in Southern dishes. The smoked meat creates a rich broth that infuses the greens with deep, savory flavors, transforming simple wild vegetables into a robust side dish that perfectly complements the heartiness of Corn Dodgers.

INGREDIENTS

2 bunches greens (collards, turnip greens, or kale)
1 tablespoon rendered bacon fat (see page 80)
1 small yellow onion, chopped
2 garlic cloves, finely chopped
1 bone-in smoked ham hock
4 cups chicken stock

Thoroughly wash the greens. For collards, wash each leaf individually to remove the grit. Kale and other tender greens only need a light rinse.

Tear the leaves into 1- to 2-inch pieces, discarding the stems.

Heat a large Dutch oven over medium heat for 1 minute.

Add the bacon fat and onion and sauté or 1 minute, stirring once.

Add the garlic and cook for 2 more minutes, stirring once.

Add the greens, smoked ham hock, and chicken stock. Cover and simmer.

Kale can be removed after 20 minutes, whereas collards and turnip greens will need 1 hour to cook to become tender and absorb the flavors.

SERVES
4 OR 5

Slow-Cooked Soup

The meal which awaited us was as unlike the first supper we had there enjoyed as possible. My wife had improvised a table of a board laid on two casks, on this was spread a white damask tablecloth, on which were placed knives, forks, spoons and plates for each person. A tureen of good soup first appeared, followed by a capital omelette, then slices of the ham; and finally some Dutch cheese, butter and biscuits, with a bottle of the captain's canary wine, completed the repast.

—JOHANN WYSS, *THE SWISS FAMILY ROBINSON*

A Swiss family bound for Australia finds themselves shipwrecked on a remote, uninhabited island in the East Indies. Despite their isolation, the Robinson family adapts, using a mix of salvaged and locally sourced ingredients to sustain themselves, reflecting the era's curiosity toward exploring other worlds. Draw inspiration from their resourcefulness and combine these ingredients to create a rich soup full of flavor. Use a good-quality beef broth to form the base in place of "portable soup"—a concentrated broth typically carried on ships for long voyages. Smoked ham hock infuses the soup with robust flavor, whereas the egg yolks are essential to transform the broth into a velvety, rich soup. But temper the eggs carefully before gradually introducing them to the hot broth to avoid curdling.

INGREDIENTS

¼ cup olive oil
1 large onion, finely chopped
2 teaspoons dried thyme
1 pound bone-in smoked ham hock
1 cup beef broth
1 teaspoon ground black pepper
2 large carrots, diced
1 bay leaf
13 cups water, divided
3 large egg yolks

In a 7-quart Dutch oven, heat the olive oil over medium heat for 2 minutes. Add the onion and thyme and sauté for 4 minutes, stirring occasionally.

Add the smoked ham hock, beef broth, pepper, diced carrots, bay leaf, and 11 cups of water. Cover the pot and bring to a boil over medium-low heat.

Partially uncover the pot, shift the lid ever so slightly ajar, reduce the heat to low, and simmer for 2 hours until the meat easily pulls off the bone. Add another 2 cups of water halfway through cooking.

Turn off the heat and carefully remove the bone and meat from the pot. Scoop out 1 cup of the broth and let it cool for 5 minutes.

In a medium bowl, whisk the egg yolks into the cooled broth, then slowly pour the mixture back into the pot, whisking constantly for 1 minute to incorporate. Shred the ham and return it to the soup.

Gently heat the soup for 3 minutes more, stirring constantly to thicken the soup slightly before serving.

To store leftovers, let the soup cool for 30 minutes before transferring it to an airtight container and placing it in the refrigerator. Use within 3 days.

PAIRS WELL WITH: Serve hot with Dutch cheese, butter, and your choice of biscuits, such as *Black Beauty*–inspired Oat Cakes (page 62) or *The Railway Children*–inspired A Welcome Supper biscuits (page 91).

MAKES
8 PIECES

Croûte au Fromage

. . . the old man held a large piece of cheese on a long iron fork over the fire, turning it round and round till it was toasted a nice golden yellow color on each side. Heidi watched all that was going on with eager curiosity.

Then he brought her a large slice of bread and a piece of the golden cheese and told her to eat . . .

". . . you must have some more," and the old man filled her bowl again to the brim [with milk] and set it before the child, who was now hungrily beginning her bread having first spread it with the cheese, which after being toasted was soft as butter; the two together tasted deliciously, and the child looked the picture of content as she sat eating, and at intervals taking further draughts of milk.

—JOHANNA SPYRI, *HEIDI*

Heidi has lived with her aunt since being orphaned, but when her aunt is unable to care for her any longer, Heidi is sent to live with her reclusive grandfather in the picturesque Swiss Alps. Amid the rolling fields and rugged peaks, her grandfather prepares a simple yet satisfying meal that emulates the rustic fare of mountain life—cheese on toast, a Swiss staple, also known as Croûte au Fromage. Serve with a hearty bread that you might find in the region, like rye or a mixed grain, to complement the rich, melted traditional Swiss cheeses like Gruyère, raclette (Swiss), or Emmental all with a nutty, earthy flavor.

INGREDIENTS

1 pound semihard cheese (use a combination of Swiss, Gruyère, and Emmental), grated
3 large eggs
2 tablespoons mustard (medium spice)
¾ cup dry white wine, divided (see note)
8 slices rye bread
¼ cup unsalted butter, divided

CHEFS IN THE MAKING

AGES 5–10: Practice grating cheese with a box grater with supervision.

Place bread slices onto a tray for the oven method and help spoon the cheese mixture evenly on top.

In a medium bowl, combine the grated cheese, eggs, mustard, and ¼ cup of wine. Mix until smooth. Spread the cheese mixture evenly across the slices of rye bread.

TO MAKE ON THE STOVE: In a 9-inch heavy-bottomed frying pan over medium-low heat, melt 1 tablespoon of butter and add 2 tablespoons of wine.

Place two bread slices in the pan, cheese side up. Cover with a lid. Cook for 5 minutes, until the cheese has melted completely.

Serve immediately and repeat the steps with the remaining butter, wine, and bread slices.

TO MAKE IN THE OVEN: Preheat the oven to 375°F.

Melt the butter in the oven on a sheet pan for 2 minutes. Pour in the remaining ½ cup of wine and swirl on the pan to spread.

Arrange all the bread slices on the sheet pan, cheese side up. Bake for 12 minutes, until the cheese has melted completely. Serve immediately.

NOTE: To adapt this age-old recipe for young families, replace the white wine with apple cider vinegar.

MAKES ONE 9-INCH PIE

Poultry Pie

So a big pigeon pie was brought in and put on a sidetable, and I made a hearty supper, for I was as hungry as a hawk, while Mr. Dance was further complimented and at last dismissed.

—ROBERT LOUIS STEVENSON, *TREASURE ISLAND*

Swashbuckling adventures are just beginning for young Jim Hawkins, who helps his mother run the Admiral Benbow Inn. When the pirate Captain Flint arrives, ruthless pirates soon follow, searching for an oilskin packet of papers. After startling events, Jim, with the help of Supervisor Dance, hurries to place them safely with Dr. Livesey, the town physician and magistrate, and Squire Trelawney, a wealthy landowner. Before the papers are explored, where an old treasure map will soon be discovered, Jim hungrily finds solace in a hearty meal of the era—pigeon pie. For contemporary cooks, chicken provides a more accessible alternative to pigeon, whereas adding leeks to the pie extends the filling, making this classic dish both satisfying and suitable for modern palates.

SHORTCRUST PASTRY

2 cups all-purpose flour, plus more for dusting
½ teaspoon sea salt
½ cup cold unsalted butter, chopped into ¾-inch cubes, plus more for the pan
¼ cup cold water

FILLING

2 cups diced chicken thigh meat
¼ teaspoon sea salt
1¼ teaspoons ground black pepper, divided
1 large leek
6 tablespoons unsalted butter, divided
3 garlic cloves, minced
1 yellow onion, chopped
1 tablespoon apple cider vinegar
2 cups cubed (½ inch) red potatoes
1½ cups chicken stock
1 bay leaf
4 thyme sprigs or ½ teaspoon dried thyme
1½ cups heavy cream
3 tablespoons all-purpose flour

SPECIAL EQUIPMENT

Pie weights

TO MAKE SHORTCRUST PASTRY: In a food processor, combine the flour and sea salt and pulse to combine. Turn on the processor and add the cold unsalted butter cubes. Pulse for 10 seconds until the flour and butter combine into a wet crumb.

With the processor running, pour the cold water in a steady stream through the tube feeder until the dough forms into a ball. Wrap the dough tightly in parchment paper and place it in the refrigerator for 1 hour.

TO MAKE THE FILLING: Preheat the oven to 400°F. Season the chicken thighs with the sea salt and ¼ teaspoon of pepper.

Slice the leek in half lengthwise and thoroughly wash the dirt from between the leaves. Finely slice the leek (it yields about 4 cups when packed). Separate the dark and white leaves.

In a large frying pan, melt 3 tablespoons of butter over medium-low heat. Sauté the green parts of the leek for 5 minutes.

Add the white parts of the leek, the garlic, and onion and continue sautéing for another 5 minutes until soft. Remove from the pan and set aside.

Add the remaining butter to the pan and let it melt. Add the diced chicken thighs and spread to cover the base of the pan. Cook for 2 to 3 minutes to sear, stirring halfway through.

Add the apple cider vinegar and use a wooden spoon to scrape the bottom of the pan to loosen any browned bits.

Add the cubed potatoes and cook for 5 minutes, stirring occasionally. Add the chicken stock, bay leaf, and thyme. Cover and cook for 10 minutes.

Return the leeks to the pan and stir. Add the heavy cream and the remaining 1 teaspoon of pepper. Sprinkle the flour over the mixture and stir well.

Continued on page 90

FACT NOT FICTION

In the United Kingdom, pigeon pie signified a meal of higher social standing for centuries due to the need for dovecotes to house the pigeons, reflecting the status of Dr. Livesey and Squire Trelawney.

Cook for an additional 5 minutes until the sauce thickens. Remove from the heat, cool slightly, and remove the bay leaf.

Butter and flour a 9-inch shallow pie plate. Roll out two-thirds of the pastry and line the pie plate, allowing excess to drape over the edges. Trim the dough.

Line the pastry with parchment paper and fill the base with pie weights, dried beans, or rice. Prebaking the crust ensures the crust is cooked and avoids it becoming soggy, whereas the weights or beans prevent the pastry from puffing up. Bake for 10 minutes.

Remove from the oven, take out the weights and paper, and spoon the filling into the pastry.

Roll the remaining pastry and cover the pie to form a lid. Press down the edges and trim the excess pastry. Pierce the top three times with a knife to allow steam to escape. Bake for 25 minutes, until the pastry top is golden brown.

Let the pie cool slightly before serving with a fresh salad. To store, let the pie cool before placing in an airtight container in the refrigerator for 3 days.

MAKES 25 MARIE BISCUITS PLUS 45 PLAIN BISCUITS

A Welcome Supper

Everyone was very, very tired, but everyone cheered up at the sight of the funny and delightful supper. There were biscuits, the Marie and the plain kind, sardines, preserved ginger, cooking raisins, and candied peel and marmalade. [...] ginger wine and water, out of willow-patterned tea-cups, because the glasses couldn't be found.

—EDITH NESBIT, *THE RAILWAY CHILDREN*

After moving to a country house near a railway due to their father's mysterious absence, three children and their mother make the best of their new circumstances and on their first night assemble an unusual supper that lifts everyone's spirits. Making do with what's at hand, this patchwork of treats is an eclectic array of items. To re-create this meal at home, delve into your pantry for leftovers from other recipes in this cookbook: Use extra candied peel from *The Velveteen Rabbit's* Orange and Chocolate Almond Cookies (page 106), leftover raisins from Hook's Rich (Fruit) Cake (page 103), and remaining marmalade from Orange Marmalade Scrolls (page 13). The Marie biscuit recipe—a light, slightly sweetened cookie perfect for tea or coffee—pairs well with the sweet accompaniments, whereas the plain biscuits (saltine crackers) make a simple base for the sardines or any savory leftovers.

MARIE BISCUITS

¼ cup whole milk
¼ cup granulated sugar
1 teaspoon vanilla extract
½ teaspoon baking powder
1⅓ cups all-purpose flour
¼ teaspoon sea salt
2 tablespoons cold unsalted butter

PLAIN BISCUITS

1 cup all-purpose flour, plus more for dusting
1 teaspoon sea salt, divided
¼ cup vegetable oil, divided
⅓ cup water

TO MAKE THE MARIE BISCUITS: Preheat the oven to 350°F.

In a heatproof measuring cup, combine the milk and granulated sugar and microwave on 100 percent power for 30 seconds to heat. Stir to dissolve the sugar. Whisk in the vanilla and then whisk in the baking powder for 30 seconds.

In a food processor, pulse together the flour and the sea salt. Add the cold butter and pulse for 30 seconds until a wet crumb forms, then pour in the wet ingredients. Pulse for 30 seconds until a dough forms.

Roll out the dough until ⅛ inch thick and cut out circles using a 2½-inch cookie cutter. Transfer the cookies to an unlined baking sheet and pierce five lines down the center of each cookie using a fork.

Bake for 12 minutes until lightly golden. Remove from the oven and let the cookies cool for 5 minutes before serving. Store in an airtight container at room temperature for up to 1 week.

TO MAKE THE PLAIN BISCUITS: Preheat the oven to 350°F.

In a food processor, combine the flour, ½ teaspoon of sea salt, 2 tablespoons of vegetable oil, and the water. Process for 30 seconds until the dough forms into a ball.

Dust your counter with a little flour and turn out the dough onto the counter. Cover with a kitchen towel and let rest for 10 minutes.

Using a rolling pin, roll the dough out to a 6-by-18-inch rectangle. Slice into 1½-by-2-inch pieces. Transfer the dough pieces to a baking sheet lined with parchment paper and pierce each cracker twice with a fork.

Continued on page 93

CHEFS IN THE MAKING

AGES 3–5: Prick holes using a child-safe fork into biscuits and crackers (with supervision!).

AGES 5–10: Measure dry ingredients and pour liquids into the processor.

Roll out dough and use cookie cutters to cut out shapes.

Brush oil onto crackers and sprinkle sea salt evenly.

AGES 10+: Try making these biscuits yourself! Keep an adult nearby for help with the oven as needed.

FACT NOT FICTION

In the United States, the word cookie *is generally used to describe what the British call "biscuits." Though today the word* cracker *is the common term for savory options, historically "biscuits" referred to both sweet and savory baked goods that were crisp and dry.*

Brush the remaining 2 tablespoons of vegetable oil onto the crackers using a silicone brush. Sprinkle the remaining ½ teaspoon of sea salt evenly over the crackers.

Bake on the lowest rack of the oven for 15 minutes, until the crackers are lightly golden. If the crackers brown more on one side of the pan, indicating oven hot spots, rotate the baking sheet halfway through baking.

Allow the biscuits to cool completely before storing in an airtight container for up to 1 week at room temperature.

97
Blancmange
Little Women

98
Perfectly Pollyanna Ice-Cream Sundae
Pollyanna

101
Victorian Sponge Cake with Earl Grey Whipped Cream
A Little Princess

103
Hook's Rich (Fruit) Cake
Peter and Wendy

106
Orange and Chocolate Almond Cookies
The Velveteen Rabbit

109
Bread-and-Butterfly Pudding
Through the Looking-Glass and What Alice Found There

Traditional Treats

On this the White Rabbit blew three blasts on the trumpet, and then unrolled the parchment scroll, and read as follows:--

"The Queen of Hearts, she made some tarts,
All on a summer day:
The Knave of Hearts, he stole those tarts,
And took them quite away!"

—LEWIS CARROLL, *ALICE'S ADVENTURES IN WONDERLAND*

Some of the most familiar desserts of the past have quietly disappeared from everyday tables, but their charm and deliciousness remain timeless. Many of those forgotten traditional treats that would have been staples in your favorite characters' kitchens can be found in this chapter, ready to become one of your go-to treats.

As a recipe that dates back to the eleventh century, bread pudding was a familiar sight in British kitchens and considered a favorite nursery food. It transformed stale bread into something warm and satisfying, a true comfort food. In a nod to the whimsical creatures Alice encounters in *Through the Looking-Glass and What Alice Found There*, the classic dish takes on a new enchantment as Bread-and-Butterfly Pudding (page 109), topped with a tea-infused cream.

With variations originating since medieval Europe, the Blancmange recipe (page 97) inspired by the one Meg whipped up in *Little Women*, with its delicate texture and flavor, is a forgotten gem worth reviving. The American classic that originates from the late 1800s, Perfectly Pollyanna Ice-Cream Sundae (page 98), is just the time-honored frozen treat to brighten a hot afternoon. And the recipe for Hook's Rich (Fruit) Cake (page 103), inspired by a dessert that was once a staple for a wedding as well at Christmas, now with a *Peter and Wendy*–inspired twist, is ready for an afternoon of make-believe and imagination.

From Victorian Sponge Cake with Earl Grey Whipped Cream (page 101) to Orange and Chocolate Almond Cookies (page 106), rediscover timeless delicacies and show your affection for these classic confections by preparing with, and sharing with, the loved ones in your life.

Blancmange

"Here I am, bag and baggage," she said briskly. "Mother sent her love, and was glad if I could do anything for you. Meg wanted me to bring some of her blanc mange, she makes it very nicely, and Beth thought her cats would be comforting. I knew you'd laugh at them, but I couldn't refuse, she was so anxious to do something."

It so happened that Beth's funny loan was just the thing, for in laughing over the kits, Laurie forgot his bashfulness, and grew sociable at once.

"That looks too pretty to eat," he said, smiling with pleasure, as Jo uncovered the dish, and showed the blanc mange, surrounded by a garland of green leaves, and the scarlet flowers of Amy's pet geranium."

—LOUISA MAY ALCOTT, *LITTLE WOMEN*

With their father away at war, the four March sisters—Meg, Jo, Beth, and Amy—learn to navigate hardships while being encouraged by their mother to think of others. Spotting their neighbor Laurie confined indoors with a cold, Jo resolves to lift his spirits and keep boredom at bay. She spiritedly brings her natural cheer, companionship, and her sister Meg's beautifully made Blancmange, a delicate dessert, both in flavor and texture, made with simple ingredients—milk, sugar, and gelatin—and flavored subtly with vanilla and a hint of cinnamon. Though Blancmange can be set in a basic pudding bowl, it also offers a reason to start your hunt for antique ceramic pudding molds in ornate shapes. There's no need to grease the mold. When ready to serve, let gravity do the work.

INGREDIENTS

⅓ cup cornstarch (see note)
3 cups whole milk, divided
½ cup raw sugar
1 teaspoon vanilla extract
½ teaspoon ground cinnamon

SPECIAL EQUIPMENT

2½-cup pudding mold

In a small bowl, whisk together the cornstarch and ½ cup of milk to form a smooth paste. Then whisk in another 1½ cups of milk. Set aside.

Pour the remaining 1 cup of milk into a medium saucepan. Place it over medium-low heat and cook for 2 minutes, bringing it to a simmer. Stir in the raw sugar for 1 minute to dissolve.

Slowly pour the cornstarch mixture into the warm milk in a slow, steady stream, whisking constantly to prevent lumps.

Scoop some of the warm milk from the pot back into the bowl or jug used for the cornstarch mixture to loosen any remaining sugar, then pour it back into the saucepan.

Continue cooking the mixture for another 5 minutes, whisking every minute until the sauce thickens to your desired consistency.

Turn off the heat and whisk in the vanilla and cinnamon. Pour the mixture into a 2½-cup mold.

Cover with a plate and refrigerate the pudding for 6 hours until fully set. Once set, remove the pudding from the mold and serve. Consume within 3 days for the best taste and texture.

NOTE: This recipe can easily be made gluten-free! Be sure to use a certified gluten-free cornstarch, as some brands may contain traces of gluten.

MAKES
4 SUNDAES

Perfectly Pollyanna Ice-Cream Sundae

"I'm so glad. It must be perfectly lovely to have lots of money. I never knew any one that did have, only the Whites—they're some rich. They have carpets in every room and ice-cream Sundays. Does Aunt Polly have ice-cream Sundays?"

—ELEANOR H. PORTER, *POLLYANNA*

In a small town in New England, Pollyanna, an eleven-year-old orphan, finds a new home with her Aunt Polly. Known for her strict and stern approach to life, her aunt is in stark contrast to Pollyanna's boundless optimism and cheerful disposition. Just as Pollyanna's infectious enthusiasm brings a new light to her town, serving up an ice-cream sundae can create a simple joyous moment. The ice-cream sundae, an American invention that became popular just decades before *Pollyanna* was written, began with an impromptu drizzle of chocolate syrup, typically used for sodas, before evolving with nuts, fruit sauces, and whipped cream. For an old-fashioned touch, top classic vanilla ice cream with this homemade cherry sauce and serve in an iconic tulip-shaped glass.

CHERRY SYRUP

2 cups pitted cherries
1¼ cups granulated sugar
½ cup water
⅓ cup fresh lemon juice
¼ teaspoon sea salt
1/16 teaspoon ground white pepper
2 teaspoons cornstarch (see note)
1 teaspoon vanilla extract

ICE-CREAM SUNDAES

4 cups vanilla ice cream
Cherry syrup
1 cup whipped cream
½ cup crushed roasted peanuts
4 maraschino cherries

TO MAKE THE CHERRY SYRUP: In a medium saucepan, combine the cherries, sugar, water, lemon juice, sea salt, white pepper, and cornstarch over medium heat.

Cook for 10 minutes, stirring occasionally, then reduce the heat to medium low and continue cooking for 35 minutes, until the syrup has thickened and turned a glossy, deep red. To check for doneness, dip a spoon into the syrup and let it cool for a minute. The syrup will coat the back of the spoon without running off like liquid.

Mash the cherries with a potato masher, then pour the mixture through a fine-mesh strainer into a large heatproof bowl, pressing the cherries to release all their juices. Use a wooden spoon to scrape the underside of the strainer. Stir in the vanilla.

Let cool for 15 minutes, then pour into an airtight container and place in the refrigerator for 30 minutes to cool before using. Store for up to 2 weeks.

TO MAKE THE ICE-CREAM SUNDAES: In each sundae glass, place 2 scoops of vanilla ice cream. Evenly drizzle homemade cherry syrup over the ice cream and top with whipped cream. Sprinkle each sundae with 2 tablespoons of crushed roasted peanuts and a maraschino cherry on top to finish.

NOTE: This recipe can easily be made gluten-free! Be sure to use a certified gluten-free cornstarch, as some brands may contain traces of gluten.

CHEFS IN THE MAKING

AGES 3–5: Help scoop the ice cream into glasses.

AGES 5–10: Drizzle the cooled cherry syrup over the ice cream and help top the sundaes with whipped cream and crushed peanuts.

MAKES ONE 7-INCH CAKE

Victorian Sponge Cake with Earl Grey Whipped Cream

"No one is anywhere about," she explained. "If your bedrooms are finished, perhaps you might stay a tiny while. I thought—perhaps—you might like a piece of cake."

The next ten minutes seemed to Becky like a sort of delirium. Sara opened a cupboard, and gave her a thick slice of cake. She seemed to rejoice when it was devoured in hungry bites. She talked and asked questions, and laughed until Becky's fears actually began to calm themselves, and she once or twice gathered boldness enough to ask a question or so herself, daring as she felt it to be.

—FRANCES HODGSON BURNETT, *A LITTLE PRINCESS*

Daughter of a wealthy English widower who spoils her endlessly, Sara Crewe extends generosity and kindness to all around her, regardless of their station. The thick slices of cake she shares with Becky, a scullery maid at Miss Minchin's boarding school, might have been a Seed Cake like the one seen in *The Secret Garden* (page 57) or this Victorian sponge cake. In the United States, this cake is often referred to as a pound cake, named for the equal weight of its key ingredients: eggs, butter, sugar, and flour. This adaptation is scaled down to create a more intimate serving and, in a nod to traditional British teatime, whipped cream is infused with citrusy flavors of Earl Grey tea.

TEA-INFUSED CREAM

½ cup heavy cream
1 teaspoon loose-leaf Earl Grey tea
¼ cup mascarpone cream
½ cup powdered sugar

SPONGE CAKE

1 cup unsalted butter, room temperature, plus more for greasing
1 cup granulated sugar
1 teaspoon vanilla extract
3 large eggs, room temperature
2 cups all-purpose flour, plus more for dusting
½ teaspoon sea salt

TO MAKE THE TEA-INFUSED CREAM: In a microwave-friendly bowl, heat the heavy cream in the microwave on 100 percent power for 50 seconds, then stir in the tea leaves. Let the cream sit for 1 hour to infuse, then place it in the refrigerator overnight (or at least 4 hours to fully infuse).

Strain the cream through a fine-mesh strainer into the bowl of a stand mixer, or a large mixing bowl if using a hand mixer, using the back of a spoon to help the cream through. Add the mascarpone and powdered sugar and whisk for 2 minutes until stiff peaks form.

The cream can be prepared in advance and stored in the refrigerator for up to 2 days in an airtight container.

TO MAKE THE SPONGE CAKE: Preheat the oven to 400°F. Butter and flour a 7-inch round cake pan.

In the stand mixer bowl, or a large mixing bowl if using a hand mixer, beat together the butter and granulated sugar for 2 minutes until light and fluffy, scraping down the bowl halfway through. Add the vanilla and then the eggs one at a time, beating for 1 minute between each addition.

In a small bowl, stir together the flour and sea salt, then sift the dry ingredients into the wet mixture. Stir until just combined to avoid condensing the cake batter. Pour the batter into the prepared pan and smooth the top.

Continued on page 102

Bake for 10 minutes, then reduce the heat to 350°F and continue baking for 55 minutes, until a skewer inserted into the center of the cake comes out clean.

Allow the cake to cool in the pan for 15 minutes before removing. Either serve the cream on the side or slice the cake in half horizontally and fill it with the tea cream before serving.

NOTE: You'll notice there's no baking powder in this recipe—that's not a mistake! This Victorian sponge relies on air whipped into both the creamed butter and sugar and the eggs to give it its rise, so be sure to use a stand mixer or electric hand mixer. The initial high oven temperature helps the air expand quickly and then set. This is particularly useful in the center of the cake, which can otherwise become dense. Lowering the heat helps the cake finish baking evenly without overbrowning.

CHEFS IN THE MAKING

AGES 3–5: Spread the cream between slices of the cake.

Have an adult hold a fine-mesh strainer with powdered sugar over the cake and let you tap to decorate.

AGES 5–10: Help by measuring out the ingredients for the cake and cream, including cracking the eggs into separate bowls before they are added to the cake batter.

Stir together the flour and salt, then sift into the wet mixture.

AGES 10+: Use the stand mixer to whip the tea-infused cream to stiff peaks to hold their form.

FACT NOT FICTION

Traditionally, two sponge cakes are baked, the rounded tops sliced off to level, then filled with jam and/or cream between both and lightly dusted with powdered sugar to make a Victoria Sandwich Cake. This cake was a staple of British afternoon tea that Sara, with her upbringing, could have been familiar with.

MAKES ONE 7-INCH CAKE

Hook's Rich (Fruit) Cake

"To return to the ship," Hook replied slowly through his teeth, "and cook a large rich cake of a jolly thickness with green sugar on it. There can be but one room below, for there is but one chimney. The silly moles had not the sense to see that they did not need a door apiece. That shows they have no mother. We will leave the cake on the shore of the mermaids' lagoon. These boys are always swimming about there, playing with the mermaids. They will find the cake and they will gobble it up, because, having no mother, they don't know how dangerous 'tis to eat rich damp cake." He burst into laughter, not hollow laughter now, but honest laughter. "Aha, they will die."

—J. M. BARRIE, *PETER AND WENDY*

Peter Pan and Captain Hook are sworn enemies, and their rivalry only deepens after each encounter, especially their last one, when a ticking crocodile got a taste of Hook's hand. After retelling this story to his first mate, Smee, Captain Hook finds the Lost Boys' home and schemes with a dark plot involving a rich, dangerously enticing cake. Though it is traditional to saturate fruit cake with alcohol such as rum and brandy over a time span of days or weeks to infuse the flavors and preserve the cake for Christmas and weddings, a variation using juice and marmalade creates a decadent cake that can be baked the very next day.

FRUIT CAKE

1½ cups raisins
1½ cups sultanas
1 cup currants
½ cup candied peel (see note)
¾ cup chopped nuts (pecans, walnuts)
¾ cup glacé cherries
½ cup pineapple juice
½ teaspoon almond extract
3 tablespoons fresh lemon juice
1 cup unsalted butter, room temperature, plus more for the pan
1 cup lightly packed light brown sugar
2 tablespoons marmalade
4 large eggs, room temperature
1½ cups all-purpose flour
½ teaspoon baking powder
2 teaspoons ground cinnamon
⅛ teaspoon ground allspice
⅛ teaspoon ground nutmeg
½ teaspoon sea salt

TO MAKE THE FRUIT CAKE: In a large mixing bowl, combine the raisins, sultanas, currants, candied peel, chopped nuts, and glacé cherries. Pour the pineapple juice, almond extract, and lemon juice over the mixture and stir to combine.

Cover the bowl with a plate and set aside overnight at room temperature to infuse. When ready to bake, preheat the oven to 300°F. Butter a 7-inch round cake pan and line it with parchment parchment paper.

In the bowl of a stand mixer, or a large mixing bowl if using a hand mixer, cream together the butter and brown sugar on medium speed for 2 minutes. Scrape down the sides of the bowl, then mix in the marmalade and eggs until well combined.

In a large bowl, sift together the flour, baking powder, cinnamon, allspice, nutmeg, and sea salt.

To the bowl of the stand mixer, alternate adding the fruit mixture and the flour mixture a bit at a time until all is added and combined.

Scoop the batter into the prepared cake pan. Smooth the surface of the batter in the pan.

Bake for 2 hours 45 minutes, when a skewer inserted into the center of the cake comes out clean. Allow the cake to cool in the pan for 1 hour before turning it out onto a wire rack.

Continued on page 105

PISTACHIO MARZIPAN

½ cup shelled pistachios
1 cup fine almond meal
1 large egg white
2 teaspoons lemon extract
1 cup powdered sugar
2 drops green food coloring (optional)

ICING

1¼ cups powdered sugar
¼ teaspoon cream of tartar
2 tablespoons water

OPTIONAL DECORATION

¼ cup granulated sugar
2 or 3 drops green food coloring

TO MAKE THE PISTACHIO MARZIPAN: Combine the pistachios and almond meal in a food processor and pulse until the pistachios are ground down. Add the egg white, lemon extract, powdered sugar , and green food coloring (if using) and pulse until a dough is formed. The dough should hold form but not be sticky.

TO MAKE THE ICING AND ASSEMBLE: Make the icing: In a small bowl, whisk together the powdered sugar, cream of tartar, and water to form a thick icing. Spread over the top of the fruit cake to create a smooth finish and fill in any lumps and dips in the top of the cake. Set aside to dry at room temperature for 1 hour.

Roll out the pistachio marzipan and use an 8-inch plate and a knife to cut out a circle. Place the marzipan over the top of the cake and gently press down. Gently dampen the edges and use a knife to smooth the edges.

FOR AN OPTIONAL EXTRA DECORATION: For a festive touch, mix two or three drops of green food coloring into the granulated sugar, stirring until the color is evenly distributed. Sprinkle over the top of the cake for a decorative, sugary finish.

After serving, store by slicing the fruit cake into portions, then wrap the cake in parchment paper, then aluminum foil, and freeze for up to 3 months. Remove slices as needed and allow them to thaw at room temperature before serving. Freezing then thawing marzipan and icing will cause them to be sticky but still delicious!

NOTE: Candied citrus peel is most commonly available during the holiday season. If unavailable, you can make your own using the candied peel recipe featured in Orange and Chocolate Almond Cookies (page 106) but stop before the final step of coating it in sugar, for a stickier version. Alternatively, substitute with a mixture of freshly grated orange and lemon zest to make ¼ cup.

MAKES
24 COOKIES

Orange and Chocolate Almond Cookies

There were other things in the stocking, nuts and oranges and a toy engine, and chocolate almonds and a clockwork mouse, but the Rabbit was quite the best of all.

—MARGERY WILLIAMS, *THE VELVETEEN RABBIT*

Christmas morning brings many treasures for a young boy—some nestled within a stocking, like the velveteen rabbit, a gift that, with time and love, becomes something truly real. To capture the magic of Christmas morning, these twice-baked cookies are inspired by the stocking's delicious contents. Filled with almonds and candied orange peel and drizzled with dark chocolate—a deliberate choice, as dark chocolate helps the orange citrusy flavors pop better than milk chocolate—these twice-baked cookies make a delicious, thoughtful gift of their own.

CANDIED PEEL

4 large organic navel oranges, washed

Tip: Navel oranges are best, as they are firm enough to peel.

6½ cups water, divided
1½ cups granulated sugar, divided

COOKIES

2 large eggs, room temperature
¾ cup granulated sugar
¼ cup unsalted butter, room temperature
½ teaspoon almond extract
2 cups all-purpose flour, plus more for dusting
1½ teaspoons baking powder
½ teaspoon sea salt
1¼ cups chopped candied orange peel, divided
1 cup whole almonds
3 ounces (16 squares) dark chocolate

TO MAKE THE CANDIED PEEL: Use a vegetable peeler to peel the oranges. Try to avoid gouging too deeply into the orange, though some white pith remaining on the peel is fine.

Slice the peeled rinds into thin strips, about ¼ inch wide. It's easier to slice before cooking, as they become slippery and difficult to cut after cooking.

Place the orange peels in a medium saucepan and cover with 2 cups of water. Bring to a boil for 5 minutes over medium heat, then boil the orange peels for 10 minutes, stirring occasionally.

Drain the water and refill the pan with another 2 cups of fresh water. Bring to a boil again and cook the peels for 10 minutes, stirring occasionally. Repeat this process once more with another 2 cups of fresh water. This boiling process is repeated to help remove the bitter taste from the peels.

Tip: Don't skip the number of boiling steps, as you want to keep using fresh water to remove any bitterness.

After the final drain, return the peels to the saucepan without water. Add 1 cup of sugar and the remaining ½ cup of water to the peels. Cook over medium-low heat, stirring every 2 to 3 minutes, for 15 minutes.

Reduce the heat to low and continue cooking for another 15 minutes, stirring occasionally, until most of the sugar has condensed and formed a syrup.

In an airtight container, combine the remaining ½ cup of sugar and just the cooked orange peels and stir to coat them evenly with sugar, breaking up any clumps so each peel is individually coated. Let sit for 5 minutes, then stir again to evenly coat.

Store the candied peel in the airtight container at room temperature. It will keep for up to 1 month.

Continued on page 108

CHEFS IN THE MAKING

AGES 3–5: Help with rolling the dough into logs.

Sprinkle the candied orange peel over the cookies after glazing.

AGES 5–10: Use a vegetable peeler to peel oranges.

Measure and add the sugar and water to the saucepan before an adult completes cooking the peels.

Roll the dough into logs and place them on the baking sheet.

Help drizzle the melted chocolate over the cooled cookies.

AGES 10+: Try your hand at tempering the chocolate using the double boiler method and drizzle over the cookies.

TO MAKE THE COOKIES: Preheat the oven to 375°F. Line a baking sheet with parchment paper.

In the bowl of a stand mixer, or a large mixing bowl if using a hand mixer, whisk together the eggs and sugar on medium speed for 2 minutes until thick and light. With the mixer still running, add the butter and almond extract and mix until well combined.

In a separate large bowl, sift together the flour, baking powder, and sea salt. Gradually add the dry ingredients to the wet mixture and stir until combined. Add 1 cup of candied orange peel and the whole almonds, stirring until fully incorporated. Let the dough sit for 5 minutes to firm up.

Lightly dust a countertop with flour and turn out the dough. Dust the top of the dough with flour and roll it into two logs that are 12 inches long, 2 inches wide, and 1 inch high.

Place the logs on the prepared baking sheet and bake for 25 minutes on the middle rack of the oven, until the logs are golden brown. Remove from the oven and let cool for 30 minutes.

Lower the oven temperature to 350°F.

Use a serrated bread knife to slice the logs into 1-inch-thick slices and place them face up on the baking sheet.

Bake the cookies for 15 minutes. Flip the cookies over and bake for another 10 minutes. Remove from the oven and let cool for 10 minutes.

Fill a small saucepan with about 1 cup of water and heat over medium-low heat. Place a heatproof glass bowl over the saucepan to create a double boiler, ensuring the bowl sits above the water without touching it.

Add half the chocolate to the bowl and gently heat, stirring occasionally, until just melted.

Remove the bowl from the heat and add the remaining chocolate. Stir briskly until fully melted and slightly cooled.

Drizzle the tempered chocolate over the cookies and sprinkle with the remaining ¼ cup of chopped candied orange peel.

Let the chocolate set completely before serving. Setting time varies depending on room temperature, typically 20 to 30 minutes at 65°F to 70°F. Store in an airtight container at room temperature for 1 week.

NOTES: This recipe is written so that there is no need to use a thermometer. However, technically, to temper the chocolate correctly, the temperature should reach 115°F to 120°F. Then add the remaining chocolate and stir quickly to melt the chocolate and bring the temperature down to 90°F.

Bread-and-Butterfly Pudding

"Crawling at your feet," said the Gnat (Alice drew her feet back in some alarm), "you may observe a Bread-and-Butterfly. Its wings are thin slices of Bread-and-butter, its body is a crust, and its head is a lump of sugar."

"And what does it live on?"

"Weak tea with cream in it."

—LEWIS CARROLL, *THROUGH THE LOOKING-GLASS AND WHAT ALICE FOUND THERE*

Alice steps through a mirror into another fantastical world beyond, where everything is reversed like a reflection, even logic. Here, she encounters myriad peculiar characters and creatures, from the snap-dragonfly with its body of plum pudding that feasts on frumenty and mince pie, to the Bread-and-Butterfly Pudding. A traditional English bread-and-butter pudding is a simple dessert, crafted for centuries as a practical yet delicious way to repurpose leftover bread. Stale bread is soaked in sweetened milk, scattered through with currants, and baked. Reimagined with a modern twist, the cream is infused with an English breakfast tea.

TEA-INFUSED CREAM

- 1 cup cold heavy cream
- 2 extra-strength or 4 regular-strength English breakfast tea bags
- ½ cup cold mascarpone cheese
- 1 cup powdered sugar

BREAD PUDDING

- 2½ cups whole milk
- ⅓ cup raw sugar
- 4 large eggs, room temperature
- 7 tablespoons unsalted butter, room temperature, plus more for the baking dish
- 8 slices stale thick whole wheat bread
- 1 cup currants

TO MAKE THE TEA-INFUSED CREAM: In a microwave-friendly bowl, heat the heavy cream in the microwave for 50 seconds on 100 percent power. Tear open the tea bags and stir in the tea leaves.

Let sit for 1 hour to infuse, then place the cream in the refrigerator overnight (minimum 6 hours).

Strain the cream through a fine-mesh strainer into the bowl of a stand mixer, or a large mixing bowl if using a hand mixer.

Add the mascarpone and powdered sugar and whisk for 2 minutes until stiff peaks form.

TO MAKE THE BREAD PUDDING: Preheat the oven to 375°F.

In a medium heatproof bowl, microwave the whole milk for 2 minutes on 100 percent power to warm. Whisk in the raw sugar until dissolved.

In another medium bowl, whisk the eggs with a fork. Slowly pour in the warm milk mixture, whisking constantly so the eggs gradually adjust to the heat. Continue whisking until smooth and combined.

Butter a 9-by-9-inch baking dish. Butter both sides of the bread slices, then cut them into roughly 2-inch squares.

Continued on page 110

Layer half the bread slices in the prepared dish, followed by half the currants and then repeat with the remaining bread and currants. Pour the egg and milk mixture evenly over the bread.

Bake for 45 minutes until the top is golden brown. Spoon the cream onto the warm pudding to serve.

NOTE: Whipped cream typically has to be used immediately but adding mascarpone while whipping helps stabilize the mixture. The mascarpone and the heavy cream must be cold, not room temperature, to form properly. Prepare the tea-infused cream recipe up to 2 days in advance of the pudding or store it with the pudding leftovers.

CHEFS IN THE MAKING

AGES 3–5: Help butter the bread slices with a child-friendly knife.

Layer the bread and currants in the baking dish.

AGES 5–10+: Just getting started with baking? This is an easy recipe to start with. Have an adult check each step as you make it yourself and have them help when placing the pan in and taking it out of the oven.

114
Marilla's Raspberry Cordial
Anne of Green Gables

117
Drink Me
Alice's Adventures in Wonderland

119
Eat Me
Alice's Adventures in Wonderland

120
Tigger's Malted Milk Shake
The House at Pooh Corner

122
Baloo's Honey Ginger Syrup
The Jungle Book

124
Mulled Apple Spice Brew
The Wind in the Willows

127
Green Lemonade
The Wonderful Wizard of Oz

Delightful Sips

Heidi lifted the bowl with both hands and drank without pause till it was empty, for the thirst of all her long hot journey had returned upon her. Then she drew a deep breath—in the eagerness of her thirst she had not stopped to breathe—and put down the bowl.

"Was the milk nice?" asked her grandfather.

"I never drank any so good before," answered Heidi.

—JOHANNA SPYRI, *HEIDI*

Some of the most memorable sips in literature break everyday rules. Steeped in magic, like the Drink Me (page 117) potion from *Alice's Adventures in Wonderland*, they remind us to continue to be curious as we explore the world. Others stem from innocent enthusiasm—like Anne Shirley mistaking bottles and serving something much stronger to her best friend instead of the sweet tartness of Marilla's Raspberry Cordial (page 114) in *Anne of Green Gables*.

A refreshing beverage may delight our taste buds as a book would enchant our minds. A glass of Green Lemonade (page 127) might be just the thing after a long journey with *The Wonderful Wizard of Oz*, whereas Baloo's Honey Ginger Syrup (page 122) brims with bright flavors that transport us to the jungles of India in *The Jungle Book*.

But at the end of the day, no matter which drink you choose, the most delightful sips are the ones shared with friends—just as Mole and Ratty know well. As they settle in by the fireside in *The Wind in the Willows*, cradling mugs of Mulled Apple Spice Brew (page 124), they remind us that the most comforting drinks, such as those in this section, are often enjoyed in good company, marking the perfect way to close the chapter on an eventful day.

MAKES
2 CUPS
SYRUP PLUS
8 GLASSES

Marilla's Raspberry Cordial

No. The sitting-room will do for you and your company. But there's a bottle half full of raspberry cordial that was left over from the church social the other night. It's on the second shelf of the sitting room closet and you and Diana can have it if you like . . .

—LUCY MAUD MONTGOMERY, *ANNE OF GREEN GABLES*

Mistakenly sent to live with Marilla and Matthew Cuthbert, siblings who had intended to adopt a boy to help with farm work, Anne Shirley's spirited and imaginative personality often brings misadventures in her new life, such as the time she mistakenly served Marilla's currant wine to her kindred spirit and best friend, Diana, instead of the raspberry cordial. Only Anne could find herself in such a predicament!

INGREDIENTS

4 cups frozen raspberries
2 cups granulated sugar
½ cup white vinegar
Water or sparkling water, for topping

In a medium saucepan over high heat, mix the raspberries, sugar, and vinegar. Let the mixture cook for 10 minutes, reducing the heat to medium low halfway, and stirring occasionally to help the sugar dissolve.

Turn off the heat, remove the saucepan, and allow the flavors to infuse and cool for 1 hour.

Set a fine-mesh strainer over a large glass bowl. Pour the raspberry mixture into the strainer. Let it strain for 1 hour, occasionally stirring and gently pressing the mixture with the back of a wooden spoon. Scrape the underside of the strainer to release any cordial gel.

To serve, pour ¼ cup of cordial into a glass and top with water or sparkling water. Stir well. Transfer the remaining cordial to a bottle and refrigerate. Store for up to 3 months.

FACT NOT FICTION

The raspberry cordial in Marilla's pantry would likely have been a raspberry vinegar cordial, also known as a shrub. Traditionally, re-creating this nostalgic, tangy drink from bygone days would take 3 days of repeated straining, allowing the raspberry and vinegar flavors to meld together. However, this stovetop shortcut will bring a bottle together in just 2 hours, preserving the vintage tradition of serving vinegar cordials.

DRINK ME
Eat me
Eat me

Drink Me

There seemed to be no use in waiting by the little door, so she went back to the table, half hoping she might find another key on it, or at any rate a book of rules for shutting people up like telescopes: this time she found a little bottle on it ("which certainly was not here before," said Alice), and tied round the neck of the bottle was a paper label, with the words "DRINK ME" beautifully printed on it in large letters.

However, this bottle was not marked "poison," so Alice ventured to taste it, and, finding it very nice (it had, in fact, a sort of mixed flavour of cherry-tart, custard, pine-apple, roast turkey, toffy, and hot buttered toast), she very soon finished it off.

—LEWIS CARROLL, *ALICE'S ADVENTURES IN WONDERLAND*

Alice's day takes a turn when she tumbles down a rabbit hole after a White Rabbit and finds herself in a room with only a small door. Stumbling upon a mysterious bottle marked DRINK ME and filled with curiosity, she samples the potion and immediately experiences its magical shrinking effects. This dessert-like sip offers a taste of Wonderland's magic without any transformative side effects. Though the peculiar flavor of roast turkey isn't included, this concoction does subtly capture an umami flavor with white miso paste.

INGREDIENTS

¾ cup pineapple juice
¾ cup cherry syrup from one 15-ounce can cherries
2 tablespoons unsalted butter
¼ cup lightly packed light brown sugar
1 teaspoon white miso paste
⅔ cup whole milk
2 drops pink food coloring

SPECIAL EQUIPMENT

4 aperitif or small cordial glasses (optional)

In a small saucepan over medium heat, stir together the pineapple juice and cherry syrup and cook for 4 minutes to bring to a simmer. Reduce the heat to medium low and cook for 20 minutes until the mixture has reduced by half. Add the butter and brown sugar, stirring until dissolved.

Add the miso paste and stir until dissolved. You may need to use the back of the spoon to smoosh the paste against the side of the pan to help break the paste apart and dissolve.

Set aside to cool for 2 to 3 minutes before pouring in the whole milk and pink food coloring. Divide among 4 small glasses to serve.

The syrup can be made 3 days in advance up to the milk stage.

Continued on page 118

CHEFS IN THE MAKING

AGES 3–5: Add premeasured milk and pink food coloring before serving.

Scoop the dough into the mini loaf cavities.

AGES 5–10: Mix the dry ingredients into the wet mixture.

Help smooth the dough in the mini loaf pan.

Press currants into the dough to spell "Eat Me."

AGES 10+: Make the full drink by yourself with adult help when monitoring the stove.

NOTE: Curiouser and curiouser! Don't be tempted to skip the miso altogether—embrace the same curiosity of Alice. The miso might seem unexpected, but it transforms a simple sugary-sweet drink into something more complex, adding a subtle, savory depth (often called umami) that enhances the flavors beautifully. But don't mix them up! Be sure to choose white miso paste, which has a delicate, slightly sweet flavor, rather than red miso, which is much stronger and saltier, which will have unexpected and unwanted results.

MAKES
8 COOKIE
CAKES

Eat Me

Soon her eye fell on a little glass box that was lying under the table: she opened it, and found in it a very small cake, on which the words "EAT ME" were beautifully marked in currants. "Well, I'll eat it," said Alice, "and if it makes me grow larger, I can reach the key; and if it makes me grow smaller, I can creep under the door; so either way I'll get into the garden, and I don't care which happens!"

—LEWIS CARROLL, *ALICE'S ADVENTURES IN WONDERLAND*

INGREDIENTS

1 cup unsalted butter, room temperature, plus more for the pan
½ cup lightly packed light brown sugar
¼ cup granulated sugar
1 teaspoon vanilla extract
1 large egg, room temperature
1½ cups all-purpose flour, plus more for the pan
1 teaspoon baking powder
½ teaspoon sea salt
½ cup currants
Icing (page 105), for decorating (optional)

Preheat the oven to 375°F.

In a large bowl, cream together the butter, brown sugar, and granulated sugar on medium speed until smooth and fluffy, then mix in the vanilla and egg until combined.

In a separate mixing bowl, whisk together the flour, baking soda, and salt, then gradually mix the dry ingredients into the wet mixture until fully combined.

Butter and flour a mini loaf baking pan. Evenly scoop dough into the cavities and smooth the tops. Press small currants into the top of the dough to spell out "Eat Me."

Bake for 15 minutes, until the mini cookie cakes are golden around the edges. Remove from the oven and allow them to cool in the pan for 10 minutes before serving. Store in an airtight container for up to 1 week.

Alternatively, bake without the currants, let cool for 20 minutes, then use icing to pipe on words and decorations before serving.

MAKES 2 MILK SHAKES

Tigger's Malted Milk Shake

"What is it?" whispered Tigger to Piglet.

"His Strengthening Medicine," said Piglet. "He hates it."

So Tigger came closer, and he leant over the back of Roo's chair, and suddenly he put out his tongue, and took one large golollop, and, with a sudden jump of surprise, Kanga said, "Oh!" and then clutched at the spoon again just as it was disappearing, and pulled it safely back out of Tigger's mouth. But the Extract of Malt had gone.

—A. A. MILNE, *THE HOUSE AT POOH CORNER*

As Roo faces his daily ordeal with "Strengthening Medicine," Tigger's curiosity bounces to the rescue, unable to resist finding out if extract of malt is what Tiggers like best. In the early 1920s, malt extract was a popular health supplement, marketed for its rich vitamin B content, which can help with boosting energy. Certainly not what Tigger needs! When eaten straight, it's thick, syrupy, caramelly, and grainy, with a hint of bitterness—all flavors that may taste too complex to young ones like Roo. But with a quick rummage around the rest of Kanga's cupboard, we could find sweetened condensed milk which, when cooked together, would turn the extract into a delicious, caramelized malt sauce. When swirled into a frothy milk shake, this blend transforms into a treat so irresistible even Roo would be eager to gulp down!

CARAMEL MALT SAUCE

One 14-ounce can sweetened condensed milk

¼ cup malt extract

3 tablespoons unsalted butter, chopped

1.5 ounces (8 squares) 70 percent dark chocolate, coarsely chopped

½ teaspoon sea salt

MALTED MILK SHAKE

½ cup caramel malt sauce

1 cup whole milk

½ cup vanilla ice cream

⅛ teaspoon sea salt

TO MAKE THE CARAMEL MALT SAUCE: In a medium saucepan, combine the condensed milk, malt extract, butter, and chocolate over medium-low heat.

Heat gently, whisking constantly for 3 minutes, until the chocolate has completely melted and the mixture is smooth, before stirring in the sea salt to finish.

TO MAKE THE MALTED MILK SHAKE: In a blender, pulse together ½ cup of the caramel malt sauce, 1 cup of whole milk, ½ cup of ice cream, and the sea salt to make a very large serving or two standard milk shake servings.

Store any remaining caramel malt sauce in an airtight container in the refrigerator for up to 2 weeks.

NOTE: The sauce can be used as a sponge cake filling, or place in the microwave for 10 seconds at 100 percent power to rewarm and use as a dip for chopped fruit for a sweet snack.

CHEFS IN THE MAKING

AGES 3–5: Scoop in the ice cream and pour the milk with a grown-up's help.

AGES 5–10: Whip up the caramel malt sauce with an adult's supervision.

AGES 10+: Confident in the kitchen? Make the caramel malt sauce from scratch with adult supervision with the stove, then blend up your own milk shake, start to finish.

MALTED MILK

MAKES 1 CUP SYRUP PLUS FOUR 6-OUNCE CUPS OF TEA

Baloo's Honey Ginger Syrup

Then the only other creature who is allowed at the Pack Council—Baloo, the sleepy brown bear who teaches the wolf cubs the Law of the Jungle: old Baloo, who can come and go where he pleases because he eats only nuts and roots and honey—rose upon his hind quarters and grunted.

—RUDYARD KIPLING, *THE JUNGLE BOOK*

In the lush jungles of India, Mowgli, a young man-cub, wanders into a wolf den where Mother Wolf shields him from the fierce tiger, Shere Khan. According to the Laws of the Jungle, when a cub can stand, they must be presented at the Pack Council to be recognized and accepted. During a particularly tense council meeting, as Mother Wolf readies herself to defend Mowgli, both Baloo the bear and Bagheera the black panther step forward to speak for him, securing Mowgli's place among the pack. This syrup blends spicy ginger with the smooth sweetness of honey—both elements that Baloo would find during his foraging in the jungles of India. Poured into a hot cup of herbal tea, you'll be ready to immerse yourself in the tale of Mowgli's upbringing among the wolves.

INGREDIENTS

2 tablespoons fresh lemon juice
7 tablespoons honey
1 knob fresh ginger, sliced into 2-inch chunks
1 cup water
5 whole cloves
2 cups brewed lemongrass tea

In a small saucepan over medium-low heat, combine the lemon juice, honey, chopped ginger, water, and whole cloves. Bring the mixture to a simmer and let it cook for 5 minutes, then reduce the heat to low.

Continue to simmer for 20 minutes.

Turn off the heat and allow the mixture to cool for 1 hour.

Strain the mixture through a fine-mesh strainer into a small bowl to remove the ginger chunks and cloves. To serve, pour ¼ cup of syrup into ½ cup of lemongrass tea.

MAKES
8 CUPS

Mulled Apple Spice Brew

It did not take long to prepare the brew and thrust the tin heater well into the red heart of the fire; and soon every field-mouse was sipping and coughing and choking (for a little mulled ale goes a long way) and wiping his eyes and laughing and forgetting he had ever been cold in all his life.

—KENNETH GRAHAME, *THE WIND IN THE WILLOWS*

From impromptu picnics to warm treats for caroling field mice, the creatures of *The Wind in the Willows* are known for their warm reception. Re-create this old-time hospitality with a mulled brew to bring a cozy touch to any gathering, perfect for sipping on brisk autumn and winter evenings. *Mulled* refers to the process of heating, sweetening, and spicing a beverage. Prepared in a slow cooker, this welcoming drink can be prepared hours before your gathering begins, ready for guests as soon as they step through your door. Though traditionally mulled beverages might include wine, beer, or cider, this nonalcoholic version uses apple juice, making it a treat for guests of all ages, including the youngest of mice.

INGREDIENTS

1 bottle (64 ounces) apple juice
1 tablespoon lightly packed light brown sugar
Peel of 1 large lemon
1½ teaspoons ground cinnamon
5 whole cloves
¾ teaspoon ground ginger
3 tablespoons malt extract
2 tablespoons fresh lemon juice
3 teaspoons vanilla extract

In a slow cooker, combine the apple juice, brown sugar, lemon peel, cinnamon, cloves, ginger, and malt extract. Give the mixture a thorough stir to ensure all the ingredients are well combined.

Set your slow cooker to the low heat setting and let it simmer for 2½ hours. Stir in the lemon juice and vanilla and continue to cook for another 30 minutes. Avoid cooking for longer, as it may develop a burned taste.

Once simmered, strain through a fine-mesh strainer into a large bowl to remove any solids and serve. This brew can also be prepared the previous day, stored in the refrigerator, and reheated when ready. Use within 5 days.

MAKES
4 CUPS

Green Lemonade

Many shops stood in the street, and Dorothy saw that everything in them was green. Green candy and pop corn were offered for sale, as well as green shoes, green hats, and green clothes of all sorts. At one place a man was selling green lemonade, and when the children bought it Dorothy could see that they paid for it with green pennies.

—L. FRANK BAUM, *THE WONDERFUL WIZARD OF OZ*

Dorothy's journey in the Land of Oz leads her and her newfound friends—the Scarecrow, the Tin Woodman, and the Cowardly Lion—down the Yellow Brick Road to the Emerald City. Upon arriving, they're given green glasses that transform their view, making the city appear as though it's constructed from green marble and sparkling emeralds, transforming everything, including the food and drink, into vivid shades of green. Outside the Emerald City, Green Lemonade is possible without the need for everyone to wear green-tinted glasses when naturally colored with fresh mint.

INGREDIENTS

¼ cup loosely packed fresh mint leaves
¾ cup granulated sugar, divided
½ cup boiling water
1 cup fresh lemon juice
2 cups water (still or sparkling)
Green food coloring, for decorating (optional; see note)

Place the mint leaves in a food processor. Add half the sugar and pulse to combine.

In a separate bowl, pour the boiling water over the remaining sugar and stir to dissolve. Pour the sugar syrup and lemon juice into the food processor with the mint mixture and pulse briefly to combine.

Let the mixture sit for 20 minutes to infuse before straining the mixture through a fine-mesh strainer into a bowl to remove the mint leaves.

Top the strained mixture with the remaining 2 cups of water. Serve in glasses with ice cubes.

CHEFS IN THE MAKING

AGES 5–10: Measure, mix, and pour the lemonade yourself, but ask an adult to help with the boiling water and straining the mint.

AGES 10+: Take the reins and make this zesty lemonade from start to finish.

NOTE: Depending on your preferred texture, you can either purée the mint into a smooth paste and leave it unstrained for a grass green color or strain it for a more subtle green-yellow hue. Serve immediately, as the color will quickly fade to a muted yellow-green. For those wanting a bold shade of green, stir in 2 drops of green food coloring—or for a fun touch, hand out green-tinted sunglasses, just like the Wizard of Oz does in the Emerald City!

Suggested Menus

AFTERNOON TEA PARTY

Garden Crumpets

(The Secret Garden)

Orange Marmalade Scrolls

(Alice's Adventures in Wonderland)

Cress Sandwiches

(The Wind in the Willows)

Victorian Sponge Cake
with Earl Grey Whipped Cream

(A Little Princess)

Drink Me

(Alice's Adventures in Wonderland)

SPRINGTIME PICNIC

Mr. McGregor's Vegetable Patch Dip

(The Tale of Peter Rabbit)

Oat Cakes

(Black Beauty)

Rabbit's Savory Carrot Muffins

(Winnie-the-Pooh)

Wendy's Mammee-Apple Slice

(Peter and Wendy)

Marilla's Raspberry Cordial

(Anne of Green Gables)

SUMMER BIRTHDAY PARTY

Green Lemonade

(The Wonderful Wizard of Oz)

Coconut Pineapple Petit Fours

(The Story of Doctor Dolittle)

Cress Sandwiches

(The Wind in the Willows)

Banana Loaf

(Just So Stories)

Perfectly Pollyanna Ice-Cream Sundae

(Pollyanna)

AUTUMN HARVEST FEAST

Benjamin Bunny's
Mini Caramelized Onion Quiches

(The Tale of Benjamin Bunny)

Nutkin's Nut Loaf

(The Story of Squirrel Nutkin)

Slow-Cooked Soup

(The Swiss Family Robinson)

Paradise Picnic Pie

(What Katy Did)

WINTER BY THE FIRESIDE

Croûte au Fromage

(Heidi)

Mulled Apple Spice Brew

(The Wind in the Willows)

Orange and Chocolate Almond Cookies

(The Velveteen Rabbit)

Fry Station Safety

If you're making something that requires deep-frying, here are some important tips to prevent any kitchen fires:

- If you don't have a dedicated deep fryer, use a Dutch oven or a high-walled sauté pan.
- Never have too much oil in the pan! You don't want hot oil spilling out as soon as you put the food in.
- Only use a suitable cooking oil, such as canola, peanut, or vegetable oil.
- Always keep track of the oil temperature with a thermometer—350°F to 375°F should do the trick.
- Never put too much food in the pan at the same time.
- Never put wet food in the hot oil. It will splatter and may cause burns.
- Always have a lid nearby to cover the pan in case it starts to spill over or catch fire. A properly rated fire extinguisher is also great to have on hand in case of emergencies.
- Never leave the pan unattended and never let children near the pan.
- Never, ever put any body part in the hot oil.

Dietary Considerations

V = Vegetarian | V+ = Vegan | GF = Gluten-Free

Christmas Morning Buckwheat Pancakes **V, GF**

Orange Marmalade Scrolls **V**

English Muffins Fit for a Princess **V**

Molasses Porridge **V**

Banana Loaf **V**

Fried Egg Feast **GF**

Dorothy's Soda Bread **V**

Wendy's Mammee-Apple Slice **V**

Garden Crumpets **V**

Benjamin Bunny's Mini Caramelized Onion Quiches **V**

Currant Buns **V**

Winnie-the-Pooh's Sticky Honey Cakes **V**

Coconut Pineapple Petit Fours **V**

Crab-apple Preserve **V, V+, GF**

Cress Sandwiches and Potted Meat

Mr. McGregor's Vegetable Patch Dip **V, GF**

Seed Cake **V**

Oat Cakes **V, V+, GF**

Rabbit's Savory Carrot Muffins **V**

Paradise Picnic Pie **V**

Tappa Rolls

Bubble and Squeak **GF**

Nutkin's Nut Loaf **V**

Corn Dodgers **GF**

Greens **GF**

Slow-Cooked Soup **GF**

Croûte au Fromage **V**

Poultry Pie

A Welcome Supper **V**

Blancmange **V, GF***

Perfectly Pollyanna Ice-Cream Sundae **V, GF***

Victorian Sponge Cake with Earl Grey Whipped Cream **V**

Hook's Rich (Fruit) Cake **V**

Orange and Chocolate Almond Cookies **V**

Bread-and-Butterfly Pudding **V**

Marilla's Raspberry Cordial **V, V+, GF**

Drink Me **V, GF**

Eat Me **V**

Tigger's Malted Milk shake **V**

Baloo's Honey Ginger Syrup **V, GF**

Mulled Apple Spice Brew **V, V+**

Green Lemonade **V, V+, GF**

Measurement Conversions

CUPS	TABLESPOONS	TEASPOONS	FLUID OUNCES
1/16 cup	1 tablespoon	3 teaspoons	½ fluid ounce
⅛ cup	2 tablespoons	6 teaspoons	1 fluid ounce
¼ cup	4 tablespoons	12 teaspoons	2 fluid ounces
⅓ cup	5½ tablespoons	16½ teaspoons	2⅔ fluid ounces
½ cup	8 tablespoons	24 teaspoons	4 fluid ounces
⅔ cup	10⅔ tablespoons	32 teaspoons	5⅓ fluid ounces
¾ cup	12 tablespoons	36 teaspoons	6 fluid ounces
1 cup	16 tablespoons	48 teaspoons	8 fluid ounces

GALLONS	QUARTS	PINTS	CUPS	FLUID OUNCES
1/16 gallon	¼ quart	½ pint	1 cup	8 fluid ounces
⅛ gallon	½ quart	1 pint	2 cups	16 fluid ounces
¼ gallon	1 quart	2 pints	4 cups	32 fluid ounces
½ gallon	2 quarts	4 pints	8 cups	64 fluid ounces
1 gallon	4 quarts	8 pints	16 cups	128 fluid ounces

GRAMS	OUNCES
14 grams	½ ounce
28 grams	1 ounce
57 grams	2 ounces
85 grams	3 ounces
113 grams	4 ounces
142 grams	5 ounces
170 grams	6 ounces
283 grams	10 ounces
397 grams	14 ounces
454 grams	16 ounces
907 grams	32 ounces

FAHRENHEIT	CELSIUS
200°F	93°C
225°F	107°C
250°F	121°C
275°F	135°C
300°F	149°C
325°F	163°C
350°F	177°C
375°F	191°C
400°F	204°C
425°F	218°C
450°F	232°C

IMPERIAL	METRIC
1 inch	2.5 centimeters
2 inches	5 centimeters
4 inches	10 centimeters
6 inches	15 centimeters
8 inches	20 centimeters
10 inches	25 centimeters
12 inches	30 centimeters

About the Author

Bryton Taylor is the creator of *InLiterature*, a food blog dedicated to re-creating authentic recipes inspired by your favorite novels and children's books. Combining her love of historical cooking and reading, you'll find Bryt whipping up exquisite, sweet treats that shaped our favorite childhood tales, like Turkish Delight from Narnia inspired by *The Lion, the Witch and the Wardrobe* or honey-drenched treats from Winnie-the-Pooh's Hundred Acre Wood. Whether you're looking forward to a cozy afternoon of reading or planning your next party, Bryt helps you re-create food items just as they'd appear in your favorite books to make an unforgettable experience to savor and share.

Acknowledgments

It can be said that this cookbook was written in just a few months—and technically, that's true. But in reality, this work has been fifteen years in the making.

To those who have journeyed with me online through *InLiterature.net* (and every version before it), thank you for being part of this long and winding road as I found my niche within a niche, discovered my writing voice, and learned how to bring literary food to life. Whether you've been quietly reading from the sidelines or cheering with every new post or video I created, your presence has helped shape not only this book, but also me, creating a ripple effect that nudged me gently forward. A special mention to CJ, Emilie, Bess, Kate, and Angela for your feedback that helped shape this book.

This book has been in the caring hands of many people at Insight Editions. My heartfelt thanks to Anna and Paul, who first brought this project to me and gave me the space to play and shape it. Like a good dough, some projects need to rest before the next rise. And it seems the book was waiting for Sami, my editor, to work alongside me. Thank you for offering such thoughtful guidance and clarity to craft this cookbook into something that spans generations.

Deep thanks to Crystal for your thoroughness, making sure the recipe steps were clear and consistent and for fact-checking the historical notes with such care. To Ivy, thank you for formatting the book with precision.

And to Emma, your illustrations are pure magic and the perfect ingredient to weave nostalgia and whimsy through every page.

People come into your life at the right time, so to Julia and Sarah—thank you for guiding and teaching me how to write recipes and cookbooks these past two years. Because of you, I knew what I needed to do when I sat down to write this book, allowing me to just focus on letting creativity flow down onto paper.

I always leave the last not for the least, but for those who form my foundations.

To Sarah, thank you for bringing thorough guidance over these past few years. Using your own gifts has helped me step into mine.

To my crew—Jess, Scott, Holly, Matt, and Ron—our friendship has spanned decades and just as many themed parties. To my accountability family—Joan, Gigi, and Emily—with an extra special thanks to Holly, who has kept us showing up every month. We've seen every twist and turn of each other's lives for the past four years and what a ride it has been!

Stephen—thank you for taste-testing and being a sounding board in the early days of this book, challenging me on so many levels to drop my guard and share my creativity in its raw state. Some dances are brief, but their impact lingers long after the song ends.

To Mom and Dad—thank you for filling our childhood with stories, making books a cornerstone of our home. It has led me here.

To Madi, James, and Skye—this book is for you. I hope it inspires countless magical moments, cozy kitchens, and stories of your own as a family.

Index

A

The Adventures of Huckleberry Finn (Twain)
  Corn Dodgers, 80–82
The Adventures of Tom Sawyer (Twain)
  Fried Egg Feast, 24
Afternoon Tea Party Menu, 128
Alice's Adventures in Wonderland (Carroll)
  Drink Me, 117–118
  Eat Me, 119
  Orange Marmalade Scrolls, 13–15
Almond Cookies, Orange and Chocolate, 106–108
Anne of Green Gables (Montgomery)
  Crab-Apple Preserve, 49–50
  Marilla's Raspberry Cordial, 114
Apple Preserve, Crab-, 49
Apple Spice Brew, Mulled, 124
apricots, dried
  Wendy's Mammee-Apple Slice, 33–34
Autumn Harvest Feast Menu, 129

B

bacon
  Fried Egg Feast, 24
  Tappa Rolls, 70
bacon fat
  Corn Dodgers, 80–82
  Greens, 83
Baloo's Honey Ginger Syrup, 122
bananas
  Banana Loaf, 22
  Tappa Rolls, 70
beef
  Cress Sandwiches and Potted Meat, 54–56
Benjamin Bunny's Mini Caramelized Onion Quiches, 38–40
biscuits
  A Welcome Supper, 91–93
Black Beauty (Sewell)
  Oat Cakes, 62
Blancmange, 97
Bread-and-Butterfly Pudding, 109–110
breads and crackers
  Banana Loaf, 22
  in Bread-and-Butterfly Pudding, 109–110
  Corn Dodgers, 80–81
  in Cress Sandwiches and Potted Meat, 54–56
  in Croûte au Fromage, 86
  Currant Buns, 41
  Dorothy's Soda Bread, 26
  English Muffins Fit for a Princess, 16–18
  Garden Crumpets, 35–36
  Oat Cakes, 62
  Rabbit's Savory Carrot Muffins, 64–66
  A Welcome Supper, 91–93
Bubble and Squeak, 74–76
Buckwheat Pancakes, Christmas Morning, 10–12
Buns, Currant, 41
Butter, Yuletide, 10
buttermilk
  Corn Dodgers, 80–82

C

cabbage
  Bubble and Squeak, 74–76
cakes
  Coconut Pineapple Petit Fours, 46–48
  Hook's Rich (Fruit) Cake, 103–105
  Seed Cake, 57–59
  Victorian Sponge Cake with Earl Grey Whipped Cream, 101–102
  Winnie-the-Pooh's Sticky Honey Cakes, 44
Caramelized Onion Quiche, Benjamin Bunny's Mini, 38–40
caraway seeds
  Seed Cake, 57–59
carrots
  Rabbit's Savory Carrot Muffins, 64–66
  Slow-Cooked Soup, 84
cheddar cheese
  Benjamin Bunny's Mini Caramelized Onion Quiches, 38–40
  Nutkin's Nut Loaf, 77–78
cheese
  Benjamin Bunny's Mini Caramelized Onion Quiches, 38–40
  Croûte au Fromage, 86
  Nutkin's Nut Loaf, 77–78
  Rabbit's Savory Carrot Muffins, 64–66
cherries
  Hook's Rich (Fruit) Cake, 103–105
  Perfectly Pollyanna Ice-Cream Sundae, 98
cherry syrup
  Drink Me, 117–118
  recipe, 98
chicken
  Poultry Pie, 88
chocolate
  Orange and Chocolate Almond Cookies, 106–108
  Tigger's Malted Milk Shake, 120
Christmas Compote, 10
Christmas Morning Buckwheat Pancakes, 10–12
coconut
  Coconut Pineapple Petit Fours, 46–48
  Wendy's Mammee-Apple Slice, 33–34
coconut milk
  Tappa Rolls, 70
Compote, Christmas, 10
cookies
  Eat Me, 119
  Marie Biscuits, 91
  Orange and Chocolate Almond Cookies, 106–108
Corn Dodgers, 80– 82
corned beef
  Bubble and Squeak, 74–76
cornmeal
  Corn Dodgers, 80–82
Crab-Apple Preserve, 49
cranberries
  Christmas Compote, 10
cream
  Bread-and-Butterfly Pudding, 109–110
  Victorian Sponge Cake with Earl Grey Whipped Cream, 101–102

cream cheese
Mr. McGregor's Vegetable Patch Dip, 60
Orange Marmalade Scrolls, 13–15
Crepes, Banana, 70
Cress Sandwiches and Potted Meat, 54–56
Croûte au Fromage, 86
Crumpets, Garden, 35–36
cucumbers
Mr. McGregor's Vegetable Patch Dip, 60
Currant Buns, 41
currants
Bread-and-Butterfly Pudding, 109–110
Currant Buns, 41
Eat Me, 119
Hook's Rich (Fruit) Cake, 103–105

D

deep fryer safety, 130
desserts
Blancmange, 97
Bread-and-Butterfly Pudding, 109–110
Eat Me, 119
Hook's Rich (Fruit) Cake, 103–105
Marie Biscuits, 91
Orange and Chocolate Almond Cookies, 106–108
Paradise Picnic Pie, 67–68
Perfectly Pollyanna Ice-Cream Sundae, 98
Victorian Sponge Cake with Earl Grey Whipped Cream, 101–102
Dip, Mr. McGregor's Vegetable Patch, 60
Dorothy's Soda Bread, 26
Drink Me, 117–118
drinks
Baloo's Honey Ginger Syrup, 122
Drink Me, 117–118
Green Lemonade, 127
Marilla's Raspberry Cordial, 114
Mulled Apple Spice Brew, 124
Tigger's Malted Milk Shake, 120

E

Earl Grey Whipped Cream, Victorian Sponge Cake with, 101–102
Eat Me, 119
eggs
Benjamin Bunny's Mini Caramelized Onion Quiches, 38–40
Bread-and-Butterfly Pudding, 109–110
Croûte au Fromage, 86
Fried Egg Feast, 24
Slow-Cooked Soup, 84
English Muffins Fit for a Princess, 16–18

F

Fried Egg Feast, 24
fry station safety, 130

G

Garden Crumpets, 35–36
Ginger Syrup, Baloo's Honey, 122
Green Lemonade, 127
Greens, 83

H

ham hocks
Greens, 83
Slow-Cooked Soup, 84
hazelnuts
Nutkin's Nut Loaf, 77–78
Heidi (Spyri)
Croûte au Fromage, 56
honey
Baloo's Honey Ginger Syrup, 122
Honey Syrup, 44
Winnie-the-Pooh's Sticky Honey Cakes, 44
Hook's Rich (Fruit) Cake, 103–105
The House at Pooh Corner (Milne)
Tigger's Malted Milk Shake, 120

I

Ice-Cream Sunday, Perfectly Pollyanna, 98

J

jams and preserves
Caramelized Onion Jam, 38–40
Crab-Apple Preserve, 49
Pineapple Jam, 46–48
The Jungle Book (Kipling)
Baloo's Honey Ginger Syrup, 122
Just So Stories (Kipling)
Banana Loaf, 22

K

Ketchup, Banana, 70

L

lemons
Baloo's Honey Ginger Syrup, 122
Green Lemonade, 127
Mr. McGregor's Vegetable Patch Dip, 60
Mulled Apple Spice Brew, 124
Paradise Picnic Pie, 67–68
Rabbit's Savory Carrot Muffins, 64–66
Seed Cake, 57–59
A Little Princess (Burnett)
Currant Buns, 41–43
English Muffins Fit for a Princess, 16–18
Victorian Sponge Cake with Earl Grey Whipped Cream, 101–102
Little Women (Alcott)
Blancmange, 97
Christmas Morning Buckwheat Pancakes, 10–12

M

- Malted Milk Shake, Tigger's, 120
- mangos
  - Tappa Rolls, 70
- Marie Biscuits, 91–93
- Marilla's Raspberry Cordial, 114
- Marzipan, Pistachio, 105
- menus, 128–129
- milk
  - Blancmange, 97
  - Drink Me, 117–118
  - Tigger's Malted Milk Shake, 120
- mint
  - Green Lemonade, 127
- miso paste
  - Drink Me, 117–118
- molasses
  - Molasses Porridge, 19–21
  - Paradise Picnic Pie, 67–68
  - Yuletide Butter, 10
- Mr. McGregor's Vegetable Patch Dip, 60
- Muffins, Rabbit's Savory Carrot, 64–66
- Mulled Apple Spice Brew, 124

N

- Nutkin's Nut Loaf, 77–78

O

- Oat Cakes, 62
- oats
  - Molasses Porridge, 19–21
  - Oat Cakes, 62
  - Wendy's Mammee-Apple Slice, 33–34
- onions
  - Benjamin Bunny's Mini Caramelized Onion Quiches, 38–40
  - Nutkin's Nut Loaf, 77–78
  - Poultry Pie, 88
  - Slow-Cooked Soup, 84
- Orange and Chocolate Almond Cookies, 106–108
- Orange Marmalade Scrolls, 13–15
- oranges
  - Banana Loaf, 22
  - Christmas Compote, 10
  - Honey Syrup, 44
  - Orange and Chocolate Almond Cookies, 106–108

P

- Pancakes, Christmas Morning Buckwheat, 10–12
- Paradise Picnic Pie, 67–68
- Parmesan cheese
  - Rabbit's Savory Carrot Muffins, 64–66
- parsley
  - Mr. McGregor's Vegetable Patch Dip, 60
  - Rabbit's Savory Carrot Muffins, 64–66
- parsnips
  - Nutkin's Nut Loaf, 77–78
- passion fruit purée
  - Wendy's Mammee-Apple Slice, 33–34
- peanuts
  - Perfectly Pollyanna Ice-Cream Sundae, 98
- Pears, Poached, 19
- Perfectly Pollyanna Ice-Cream Sundae, 98
- *Peter and Wendy* (Barrie)
  - Hook's Rich (Fruit) Cake, 103–105
  - Tappa Rolls, 70
  - Wendy's Mammee-Apple Slice, 33–34
- Pie Dough, 67
- pies
  - Paradise Picnic Pie, 67–68
  - Poultry Pie, 88
- pineapple juice
  - Drink Me, 117–118
  - Hook's Rich (Fruit) Cake, 103–105
- Pineapple Petit Fours, Coconut, 46–48
- Pistachio Marzipan, 105
- Poached Pears, 19
- *Pollyanna* (Porter)
  - Perfectly Pollyanna Ice-Cream Sundae, 98
- Porridge, Molasses, 19–21
- potatoes
  - Bubble and Squeak, 74–76
  - Poultry Pie, 88
- Poultry Pie, 88–90
- puddings
  - Blancmange, 97
  - Bread-and-Butterfly Pudding, 109–110

Q

- Quiches, Benjamin Bunny's Mini Caramelized Onion, 38–40

R

- Rabbit's Savory Carrot Muffins, 64–66
- radishes
  - Mr. McGregor's Vegetable Patch Dip, 60
- *The Railway Children* (Nesbit)
  - A Welcome Supper, 91–93
- raisins
  - Hook's Rich (Fruit) Cake, 103–105
- raspberries
  - Marilla's Raspberry Cordial, 114
  - Wendy's Mammee-Apple Slice, 33–34

ricotta cheese
Benjamin Bunny's Mini Caramelized Onion Quiches, 38–40

S

sage
Nutkin's Nut Loaf, 77–78
Rabbit's Savory Carrot Muffins, 64–66
sandwiches
Cress Sandwiches and Potted Meat, 54–56
Croûte au Fromage, 86
Scrolls, Orange Marmalade, 13–15
The Secret Garden (Burnett)
Garden Crumpets, 35–36
Molasses Porridge, 19–21
Seed Cake, 57–59
Seed Cake, 57–59
Shortcrust Pastry, 38, 88
Slow-Cooked Soup, 84
Soda Bread, Dorothy's, 26
Soup, Slow-Cooked, 84
Sponge Cake with Earl Grey Whipped Cream, Victorian, 101–102
Springtime Picnic Menu, 128
The Story of Doctor Dolittle (Lofting)
Coconut Pineapple Petit Fours, 46–48
Summer Birthday Party Menu, 129
The Swiss Family Robinson (Wyss)
Slow-Cooked Soup, 54

T

The Tale of Benjamin Bunny (Potter)
Benjamin Bunny's Mini Caramelized Onion Quiches, 38–40
The Tale of Peter Rabbit (Potter)
Mr. McGregor's Vegetable Patch Dip, 60
The Tale of Squirrel Nutkin (Potter)
Nutkin's Nut Loaf, 77–78
Tappa Rolls, 70
tea
Baloo's Honey Ginger Syrup, 122
Bread-and-Butterfly Pudding, 109–110
Victorian Sponge Cake with Earl Grey Whipped Cream, 101–102
Through the Looking-Glass and What Alice Found There (Carroll)
Bread-and-Butterfly Pudding, 109–110
Tigger's Malted Milk Shake, 120
Treasure Island (Stevenson)
Poultry Pie, 88–90

V

The Velveteen Rabbit (Williams)
Orange and Chocolate Almond Cookies, 106–108
Victorian Sponge Cake with Earl Grey Whipped Cream, 101–102

W

walnuts
Hook's Rich (Fruit) Cake, 103–105
Nutkin's Nut Loaf, 77–78
watercress
Cress Sandwiches and Potted Meat, 54–56
A Welcome Supper, 91–93
Wendy's Mammee-Apple Slice, 33–34
What Katy Did (Coolidge)
Paradise Picnic Pie, 67–68
whipped cream
Perfectly Pollyanna Ice-Cream Sundae, 98
Victorian Sponge Cake with Earl Grey Whipped Cream, 101–102
The Wind in the Willows (Grahame)
Bubble and Squeak, 74–76
Cress Sandwiches and Potted Meat, 54–56
Mulled Apple Spice Brew, 124
Winnie-the-Pooh (Milne)
Rabbit's Savory Carrot Muffins, 64–66
Winnie-the-Pooh's Sticky Honey Cakes, 44
Winter by the Fireside Menu, 129
The Wonderful Wizard of Oz (Baum)
Dorothy's Soda Bread, 26–29
Green Lemonade, 127

Y

yogurt
Mr. McGregor's Vegetable Patch Dip, 60
Yuletide Butter, 10

A Treasury of Our Memories

Our favorite breakfast:

Our favorite snack:

Our favorite lunch:

Our favorite meal:

Our favorite treat:

Our favorite sip:

Notes

PO Box 3088
San Rafael, CA 94912
www.insighteditions.com

Find us on Facebook: www.facebook.com/InsightEditions
Follow us on Instagram: @insighteditions

ISBN: 979-8-88663-865-3

Publisher: Raoul Goff
SVP, Group Publisher: Vanessa Lopez
VP, Manufacturing: Alix Nicholaeff
Editorial Director: Thom O'Hearn
Art Director: Stuart Smith
Senior Designer: Brooke McCullum
Associate Editor: Sami Alvarado
Managing Editor: Shannon Ballesteros
Production Editor: Ivy Long
Production Manager: Deena Hashem
Strategic Production Planner: Lina s Palma-Temena

Illustrations by Emma Adams

Insight Editions, in association with Roots of Peace, will plant two trees for each tree used in the manufacturing of this book. Roots of Peace is an internationally renowned humanitarian organization dedicated to eradicating land mines worldwide and converting war-torn lands into productive farms and wildlife habitats. Roots of Peace will plant two million fruit and nut trees in Afghanistan and provide farmers there with the skills and support necessary for sustainable land use.

Manufactured in China by Insight Editions

10 9 8 7 6 5 4 3 2 1